AMERICAN FOLKLORE AND LEGENDS

JOHN J. MARCATANTE

GLOBE BOOK COMPANY
A Division of Simon & Schuster
Englewood Cliffs, New Jersey

Cover Art: *Deer Rattle/Deer Damcer*, Frank La Peña
Cover Design: Marek Antoniak

ISBN: 0-83590-203-0

Printed in the United States of America.
10   9   8   7   6   5   4   3   2   1

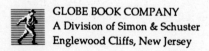
GLOBE BOOK COMPANY
A Division of Simon & Schuster
Englewood Cliffs, New Jersey

ACKNOWLEDGMENTS

The author is grateful to the following publishers, authors, and periodicals for permission to use the stories and articles listed below as source material:

Bennett, Emerson, *Mike Fink: A Legend of the Ohio*. Cincinnati, U. P. James, 1852.

Josef Berger, for special permission to use the name and character of Bowleg Bill; originated in the book *Bowleg Bill, the Sea-Going Cowboy* by Jeremiah Digges. New York, The Viking Press, 1938.

The Century Magazine and Appleton-Century-Crofts, division of Meredith Publishing Company, for permission to adapt *Pecos Bill* from "The Saga of Pecos Bill," by Edward O'Reilly, from *The Century Magazine*, October, 1923.

Dayton, Abram C., *Last Days of Knickerbocker Life in New York*. New York, George W. Harlan, 1882.

de Morgan, John, *The Hero of Ticonderoga*. Philadelphia, David McKay, copyright 1896.

Farm Journal for permission to use J. Frank Dobie's "Giants of the Southwest" from *The Country Gentleman*, Vol. XLI, 8, August 1926, as a source for ideas.

Lewis, Meriwether, *History of the Expedition Under the Command of Captains Lewis and Clark*, prepared for the press by Paul Allen. Philadelphia, Bradford and Inskeep, 1814.

Sheldon, George W., *The Story of the Volunteer Fire Department of the City of New York*. New York, Harper and Brothers, 1882.

The University of Nebraska Press for permission to adapt *Febold Feboldson* from *Febold Feboldson: Tall Tales From the Plains*, compiled by Paul R. Beath. Copyright 1955, Paul R. Beath.

Lowell Thomas, for permission to adapt stories about the Wisconsin sunlight, Connecticut trout, Florida bass, West Virginia dog, Rhode Island hen, and the fisher-hound from *Tall Stories*. Funk and Wagnalls, Inc., copyright 1931, Funk and Wagnalls, Inc.

CONTENTS

The Legends Live On   1

LOOKING EAST   9

Crispus Attucks, American Hero   11
The Daring Deed of Ethan Allen and His
   Green Mountain Boys   17
The Strange Adventure of Rip Van Winkle   23
The Headless Horseman of Sleepy Hollow   31
Johnny Appleseed's Secret   41
Joe Magarac, Mystery Man of Steel   49
Clara Barton, the Nurse Who Won Battles   57
Bowleg Bill, Cowboy of the Ocean Waves   65
Paul Bunyan and His Wonderful Blue Ox   73
      A Grab Bag of Tall Tales From the East   85

HEADING SOUTH   87

The Fountain of Youth   89
Betty Zane, the Youngest General   97
Daniel Boone and the Spirit of the Forest   105
Daniel Boone, First Detective of the Old Frontier   111
Mike Fink and the River Pirates   119
Secret Agent *M*   129
John Henry and the Monster   139
Casey Jones, Hero of the Flaming Rails   147
      A Grab Bag of Tall Tales From the South   155

RIDING WEST   157

The Courage of "Bird Woman"   159
Davy Crockett and His Fellow Heroes of the Alamo   169
Annie Oakley, Champion Sharpshooter   181

The Battle of the Two Great Warriors   187
Buffalo Bill and the Horse That Could Hunt   193
Pecos Bill, the Youth Who Tamed the West   199
The Strange Armies From the Sky   209
The Giant Who Could Solve Any Problem   215
The Celebrated Jumping Frog   223
A Tale of Flying Saucers   231
The Search for the Ranchero's Lost Treasure   243
The Heroic Chief Whose Name Was Thunder   249
        A Grab Bag of Tall Tales From the West   259

FOCUSING ON THE SELECTIONS   261

THE LEGENDS LIVE ON   263
CRISPUS ATTUCKS, AMERICAN HERO   265
THE DARING DEED OF ETHAN ALLEN AND
    HIS GREEN MOUNTAIN BOYS   266
THE STRANGE ADVENTURE OF RIP VAN WINKLE   267
THE HEADLESS HORSEMAN OF SLEEPY HOLLOW   268
JOHNNY APPLESEED'S SECRET   269
JOE MAGARAC, MYSTERY MAN OF STEEL   270
CLARA BARTON, THE NURSE WHO WON BATTLES   271
BOWLEG BILL, COWBOY OF THE OCEAN WAVES   272
PAUL BUNYAN AND HIS WONDERFUL BLUE OX   273
THE FOUNTAIN OF YOUTH   274
BETTY ZANE, THE YOUNGEST GENERAL   275
DANIEL BOONE, AND THE SPIRIT OF THE FOREST   276
DANIEL BOONE, FIRST DETECTIVE OF THE OLD FRONTIER   277
MIKE FINK AND THE RIVER PIRATES   278
SECRET AGENT M   279
JOHN HENRY AND THE MONSTER   280
CASEY JONES, HERO OF THE FLAMING RAILS   281
THE COURAGE OF "BIRD WOMAN"   282
DAVY CROCKETT AND HIS FELLOW HEROES OF THE ALAMO   283
ANNIE OAKLEY, CHAMPION SHARPSHOOTER   285
THE BATTLE OF THE TWO GREAT WARRIORS   286

BUFFALO BILL AND THE HORSE THAT COULD HUNT   287
PECOS BILL, THE YOUTH WHO TAMED THE WEST   288
THE STRANGE ARMIES FROM THE SKY   290
THE GIANT WHO COULD SOLVE ANY PROBLEM   291
THE CELEBRATED JUMPING FROG   293
A TALE OF FLYING SAUCERS   294
THE SEARCH FOR THE RANCHERO'S LOST TREASURE   296
THE HEROIC CHIEF WHOSE NAME WAS THUNDER   297
BRINGING THE STORIES TOGETHER   298

STORY THEATER   300

BETTY ZANE, THE YOUNGEST GENERAL (A RADIO SCRIPT)   301
ACTING WITHOUT WORDS   306

ix

A TOPICAL TABLE
OF CONTENTS

TALL TALES

Joe Magarac, Mystery Man of Steel   49
Bowleg Bill, Cowboy of the Ocean Waves   65
Paul Bunyan and His Wonderful Blue Ox   73
Mike Fink and the River Pirates   119
John Henry and the Monster   139
Pecos Bill, the Youth Who Tamed the West   199
The Giant Who Could Solve Any Problem   215
The Celebrated Jumping Frog   223

STRANGE ADVENTURES

The Strange Adventure of Rip Van Winkle   23
The Headless Horseman of Sleepy Hollow   31
The Fountain of Youth   89
Daniel Boone and the Spirit of the Forest   105
A Tale of Flying Saucers   231

STORIES OF FIGHTERS FOR FREEDOM

Crispus Attucks, American Hero   11
The Daring Deed of Ethan Allen and
   His Green Mountain Boys   17
Betty Zane, the Youngest General   97
Secret Agent M (Harriet Tubman)   129
Davy Crockett and His Fellow Heroes of the Alamo   169
The Heroic Chief Whose Name Was Thunder   249

Johnny Appleseed's Secret   41
Clara Barton, the Nurse Who Won Battles   57
Daniel Boone, First Detective of the Old Frontier   111
Casey Jones, Hero of the Flaming Rails   147
The Courage of "Bird Woman" (Sacajawea)   159
Annie Oakley, Champion Sharpshooter   181
The Battle of the Two Great Warriors   187
Buffalo Bill and the Horse That Could Hunt   193
The Strange Armies From the Sky   209
The Search for the Ranchero's Lost Treasure   243

GRAB BAGS OF TALL TALES

From the East   85
From the South   155
From the West   259

AMERICAN FOLKLORE AND LEGENDS

THE LEGENDS LIVE ON

Vocabulary Preview

character [*KAR ak ter*]—person in a story
Buffalo Bill is a *character* in one of our stories.

cyclone [*SY klone*]—a very strong wind
The *cyclone* went spinning along, blowing down trees, lifting the roofs off houses.

imagination [*im aj in AY shun*]—the power to see pictures in one's mind
It takes *imagination* to write a story.

lumberjack [*LUM ber jak*]—a man who cuts down trees for a living
The *lumberjack* may use an ax or a saw for his work of felling trees.

probably [*PROB ub lee*]—likely, likely to happen
Pat will *probably* be asked to be in the play.

swap [*SWOP*]—trade, give one thing for another
Bill and John *swap* books with each other when they finish reading what they have.

version [*VER zhun*]—one side of a story, a different report of the same story
Bob and Joe each told a different *version* of the tale.

2

Have you ever heard the old saying: "Too many cooks spoil the broth"? What is the meaning behind this famous statement?

Try to imagine your whole class writing a story together. Would it be right to say, "Too many authors spoil the story"? Why or why not? Might this be true of all stories that have more than one author?

Some of the stories you will read in this book have had hundreds, perhaps *thousands*, of authors. How can a single story have had thousands of authors? Read the introduction to find out.

CASEY JONES! JOHN HENRY! DAVY CROCKETT! The names of heroes like these are special to all Americans. Songs about them are sung all across the country. Stories about them reach us through books, movies and television shows.

Some stories are told a few times and then forgotten, but the tales about our great heroes never die. These wonderful stories are called *legends*. They have come down to us from early times. In fact, some of the legends were already very old when our grandparents were only children.

Perhaps you are wondering just how some of these legends came into being. The truth is that different legends got started in different ways. For instance, take the stories about Harriet Tubman. In books about the Civil War we read that she was a small woman of great courage who faced danger many times to lead her fellow slaves to freedom. She was so brave that people began to tell wonderful stories about her, just as they told exciting tales about Daniel Boone, Davy Crockett and other people.

Sometimes a storyteller stretched the truth about a hero's

deeds just a little. Sometimes he stretched the truth a mile or two or three. When the truth in a tale was stretched too far to be believable, the story became known as a *tall tale*.

Some tall tales were also made up about characters who had probably never really lived. Many of these stories may have gotten started when people began to wish out loud. For instance, there might have been an early settler in the West who wished that he could stop the terrible cyclones that often ruined his crops. Perhaps, as wishful thinking, or to make himself feel better, he may have made up the story about Pecos Bill riding the cyclone as if it were a horse.

Other stories about mighty characters who did wonderful deeds were made up or added to by people who came to America from other lands. These people brought along with them more than just the desire to do well. They brought along their own customs, ideas and, above all, their imaginations—rich, wonderful imaginations! And when these people wanted a hero to talk about, they sometimes made up one of their own.

That's probably why the settlers who came here from Hungary told their stories about Joe Magarac, the greatest steelworker of them all! They wanted everyone to know about the great things this giant worker with the Hungarian name could do for his new country. And the tales about Joe got better and better as different storytellers added details and made changes in them over the years.

Can we now begin to see why it may be said that a story can have many, many authors?

Characters like Joe Magarac and Pecos Bill pleased Americans everywhere. People liked to feel that one of their fellow countrymen, even a made-up one, could take care of any problems that might come along. And they often liked some of their heroes to be big people, so they could tell big stories about them.

Perhaps another reason why Americans liked to make some of their heroes "larger than life" was that our country is such a big place. Wide rivers! Rolling plains! Mighty mountains! Giant forests! All these are ours. And with our giant forests, it was natural to have at least one giant lumberjack like Paul Bunyan.

Some people say that there really was a Paul Bunyan. They say that he was a giant of a man who came to America from Canada. But whether or not he really lived, the stories about his great deeds live on in our legends. Even today, people enjoy making up new tales about him. These stories help to give the Paul Bunyan legend new life. In this book, you will read a brand new Paul Bunyan tale.

Another American hero who is supposed really to have lived is John Henry. The legends do not describe him as a giant. They speak of him as a man—a wonderful man who was stronger than ten ordinary men put together! This was a man with a will to work harder than any machine. Americans have always been proud to tell his story over and over again. He reminds us that a man can do just about anything he sets out to do, if his will is strong enough.

John Henry, Buffalo Bill, Ethan Allen—the list goes on and on. And the stories about our heroes go on and on, never dying out. This is because early Americans liked so much to sit around and swap stories with their friends, just as you probably do today.

Try to think what life was like, of how it was, for the American people long ago. They had no television sets or radios. Their work was hard, and when it was done they often had no special way to pass the time. So lumberjacks told each other tall tales about Paul Bunyan. Cowboys sat around their campfires and traded stories about Pecos Bill and other heroes of the West. Men who lived in towns gathered around in the local store and took turns telling story after story. And on many a warm night, neighbors sat out on their front steps and traded tales.

We know that Americans still love to hear and tell good stories, so it shouldn't surprise us to learn that in some towns a "Liar's Contest" is held each year. The winner is the person who can make up the best "whopper." (That's a polite word for any story that someone pretends is true, but really isn't.) Some people in the contests just change or add things to stories that most people already know. By doing this, these storytellers often make old tall tales grow even taller.

As you read the tall tales and other stories in this book, you may remember having heard some of them told differently. There's nothing really strange about finding different versions of the same tale. We already know that as the years went by many storytellers made changes in the old tales as they passed them along. We must also keep in mind that many of the tales have traveled around a great deal. They went from state to state and from one end of the country to the other. This happened because so many early Americans were people "on the go."

As these people moved from place to place, either to visit or settle down, they took their stories with them. The stories were then told and retold in different places by different people. And, of course, changes were made as this happened.

You can see now how many, many authors helped put

together some of the legends and folk tales we know today. Of course, when all is said and done, we don't really care if a story was developed by one author or a thousand authors. We just want that story to be good. And if it is, people will go on telling it and adding to it for years and years to come, just as they have in the past.

Looking East

CRISPUS ATTUCKS,
AMERICAN HERO

Vocabulary Preview

confusion [*con FU zhun*]—lack of order
When the fire broke out, there was *confusion* in the crowd.

furious [*FUR i us*]—very angry
John was *furious* with his friend for telling a lie.

glance [*GLANS*]—a quick look
He *glanced* up to see if anyone was looking.

harsh [*HARSH*]—hard, cruel
The boy was given a *harsh* punishment for stealing.

lobster [*LAHB ster*]—a kind of shellfish with large claws, bright red when cooked
The *lobster* crawls along under the sea.

respect [*re SPEKT*]—high opinion of someone or something
We show *respect* for our country's leaders.

serious [*SEER ee us*]—thoughtful; deep in thought
The student had a *serious* look on his face.

Nathan Hale was a young man caught spying for the Americans during the Revolutionary War. When the British captured him and found secret papers hidden in his boots, they decided to hang him immediately. Almost every American knows his famous statement before dying: "I only regret that I have but one life to lose for my country."

Nathan Hale was a true American hero. Perhaps the words "true American" are best used to describe a certain kind of person, one who believes in freedom and democracy, and who is willing to fight for them.

Such a person was Crispus Attucks. Read to find out how he proved himself to be a man of action, and not just a man of words, in the cause of American freedom.

"LOBSTERS! GET OUT OF BOSTON! Down with the British!" the angry crowd screamed at the redcoats. But the British soldiers kept on marching, their eyes straight ahead. They knew that the colonists were tired of paying high taxes to England. They also knew that the people wanted freedom from England's harsh rule.

Crispus Attucks [*KRISP us AT tuks*] and his young friend Tom, a cabin boy, stood watching the angry shouters. "Oh, Crispus," sighed Tom, "will we never drive the soldiers out? We have a right to rule our own land. Why won't they let us be free?"

"All people *want* to be free," said Crispus. "Every man would rather run his own life than have it run for him. But it isn't always easy. I should know—I was a slave when I was a boy."

Tom looked up at the seaman. "No man should be a slave! And yet no man, master or slave, is free in these colonies. We're all under England's thumb."

Crispus nodded. What Tom said was true. He took a newspaper from under his arm and showed it to the boy. Tom glanced at the paper, then threw it angrily to the ground.

"So King George plans to send a warship and more troops, does he? Well, we'll see who scares first. One day those robin redbreasts will be driven from our shores for good!"

Crispus laughed. "Redbreasts is a fine name for them," he said. Then he grew serious. The two walked on without a word for several minutes. Suddenly Crispus said, "Tom, my lad, I must help! I don't know how yet, but I must do *something* to help drive out those redcoats. There must be *something*. . . ." He stopped for a moment, thinking. Then the pair walked on down the dark street. Only their footsteps broke the silence.

Two long, unhappy years passed. The redcoats were still in the colonies, and their stay had made them even more troublesome. They demanded the best food and housing. And their treatment of the colonists grew worse and worse every day. What's more, taxes were higher than ever. The people knew that something had to happen.

Then, one night in March, 1770, something did.

Crispus Attucks and a group of friends were walking down King Street. They had been to a meeting with others who, like themselves, wanted freedom for the thirteen colonies. Suddenly they heard shouting. Seeing a crowd up the street, they broke into a run. Crispus was at their head. As he drew closer, Crispus saw that Tom was in the crowd too.

A small boy had just thrown a snowball at some redcoats standing guard before a big door. The boy was shouting,

"You jailed my father for talking against the King! Why don't you jail me too? Am I too big for you?"

The crowd laughed and shouted, but the soldiers didn't move. Just then, a small dog trotted by. Tom yelled, "Make way for the British captain!" The crowd laughed louder and louder.

An old man shook his fist in the face of a tall redcoat. "Go back to England," he cried. "Go back to King George and take your troops with you!"

The tall soldier snapped, "Be careful, old man! Show some respect for your King!"

"He shows no respect for us!" answered the old man. "He does nothing for us. All he wants is our tax money, so he can grow fatter while we pay the bills!" Another soldier warned, "Be still, you old dog, or ——."

"Or what?" broke in an angry youth. "Will you hit an old man? You must be very brave!"

The soldiers raised their guns, but even this didn't scare the people. They wouldn't be still—they had been still for too many years.

"Lobsters! Lobsters!" screamed the crowd. "King George's lobsters!"

The tall soldier shouted, "Prepare to fire!"

Suddenly Crispus and his friends jumped forward. "We've stood by for too long," he cried. "The way to rid ourselves of these soldiers is to strike back! This is our chance!"

The tall soldier roared, "Out of the way! Get off the street, in the King's name!" But Crispus, Tom and the others stood their ground.

The soldier yelled, "This is your last warning!" His face was as red as his flaming red jacket.

A young man called out, "Look at his face! He's really a lobster!" The crowd moved closer.

Just at that moment, a snowball hit the redcoat in the face.

"FIRE!" roared the furious soldier. Triggers clicked and bullets sped through the air. "FIRE!" the soldier roared again. More shouts rang out in the night.

What noise and confusion! Women screamed and fainted. Children howled as men fell bleeding to the ground. Tom saw Crispus sink to his knees. He ran to his fallen friend.

"Crispus," Tom cried. "Crispus, are you all right?"

Crispus Attucks opened his eyes and looked at the fallen men around him. "At last we've done something to help," he murmured. "Something to help ——"

The seaman didn't finish his sentence. For of the men who had been shot down on that terrible night, he was the first to die.

The awful news of how the redcoats had fired upon unarmed men spread like wildfire through the colonies. The memory of those heroes, the first to fall in the fight for liberty, stirred people's hearts and moved them to action.

A few years later, General George Washington set out to fight the redcoats. He called for men to join his army of patriots. And Tom, remembering his friend Crispus, marched proudly in that great army of the American Revolution.

THE DARING DEED OF
ETHAN ALLEN AND HIS
GREEN MOUNTAIN BOYS

Vocabulary Preview

amazement [*a MAZE ment*]—great surprise
The soldiers watched in *amazement* while the fort was taken.

dart [*DART*]—dash, run swiftly
No one should *dart* into the street without looking.

gaze [*GAZE*]—look at for a long time
Joe could *gaze* at the stars for hours.

glide [*GLIDE*]—move smoothly and quietly
Do you like to watch the skaters *glide* across the ice?

muffle [*MUF fle*]—make softer
He put his hand over his mouth to *muffle* his voice.

signal [*SIG nil*]—sign or warning to do something
The sound of the bell was the *signal* for the class to leave.

surrender [*sur REN der*]—give up
The redcoats wouldn't *surrender* their fort to anyone.

Here is a word that is hard for some people to say. Can you say it right the first time? *SHIBBOLETH*

Thousands of years ago, a man named Jephtha (*JEF tha*) used this word as a test to see which men were in his army and which were spies trying to sneak into his camp. Jephtha's men could say the word correctly, but the other men could not. The spies said *sib*boleth instead of *shib*boleth. There's no need to ask what happened to the spies!

This story is about a group of men who also had to use a password. As you read, you will discover why these men had to be so careful about their very important secret meeting.

THE MOON WAS BRIGHT in the evening sky. The woods were black and still. In the shadows, a tall, thin figure darted quickly from tree to tree. As silent as a cat, it zigzagged from hiding place to hiding place. Finally it reached the mouth of a large cave.

For a moment the stillness was broken by the soft hooting of an owl. Then, "What's the password?" called a muffled voice at the mouth of the cave. "The moon is rising," came the whispered reply.

With that, the bearded woodsman in worn buckskins slipped inside and joined the group of men talking quietly in one corner. It was a secret meeting of the Green Mountain Boys and their leader, Ethan Allen.

"Boys," Ethan was saying, "we've fought side by side in some pretty tight spots. You remember our little battle with the governor of New York Colony. That was the time he tried to take New Hampshire away from us. We taught him a good lesson!" The men grinned. They'd never forget *that* fight.

"Now I've called you to join me in something even bigger. This time we'll be fighting the British for our country's freedom! Our job is to take Fort Ticonderoga. Are you with me?"

The men looked up in amazement. What was their leader thinking of? The huge fort was loaded with cannons and hundreds of troops.

Ethan went on, "If you are with me, we strike tonight."

One of the men spoke up. "The odds are too great! The British are sure to see us. The moon is as bright as daylight."

"The British know the moon is bright as well as we do," answered Ethan. "They won't be expecting any visitors this evening. Besides, I have a plan. Well, are you with me or not, boys?"

Without a word, every man shouldered his gun and stood at attention. "I knew you wouldn't let me down," grinned Ethan. He led his men out of the cave.

The small band traveled silently through the dark woods. On and on they went until they reached the edge of Lake Champlain. There they ducked behind the thick brush lining the shore. They gazed at the huge fort across the lake.

"There are over three hundred men behind those walls," whispered Ethan. "And there are only eighty-three of us. But we're going to take that fort without firing a single shot!"

The men stirred in their hiding places. "I know what you're thinking," Ethan went on, "—that the fort has almost as many cannons as we have men. Well, you just trust me. Our plan will work."

Soon Ethan and three other men crawled down to the shore. They pulled out two boats that were hidden in the grass. Then he crept back to where the group was hiding.

"Eight more of you come with me. The twelve of us will go across in the boats and get into the fort," he said. "The rest of you wait here. Stay awake! Watch for the signal and then swim over to help."

Soon the two boats were gliding silently toward the darkest side of the fort. The men in them held leafy branches so that the boats would look like floating trees.

That night, the British guards were in a careless mood. They were sure no one would try an attack in such bright moonlight. Ethan and his men reached the fort with no trouble at all. Then they hid in the tall grass along the walls. Hour after hour passed, but they made no sound. Finally the steps of two British guards broke the stillness. One had come to replace the other at the front gate.

Suddenly, "Don't move," said a deep voice. The two guards froze in their tracks, completely surprised. "Lay down your guns," said the voice in the night. The guards tossed their rifles to the ground. Strong hands pulled them backward into the darkness.

A moment later, Ethan and his men stepped out of the shadows. Behind them lay the two guards, tied and gagged. Now the Green Mountain Boys slipped through the front gate easily. Two of the twelve crept up behind the careless soldiers on the main tower. Two others found the room where the guns were stored. Another climbed the flag tower.

Now Ethan waved his gun at the man on the flag tower. Down came the British flag, although it was raised again almost at once. But this time the flag was flying upside down! It was the signal for the others to swim across the lake.

The other six Green Mountain Boys entered the barracks, where almost three hundred soldiers lay snoring loudly. Their guns held ready, they crept around the room and waited. "These sleeping beauties are in for a big surprise," one whispered laughingly.

Ethan moved swiftly. He stepped into the bedroom of the fort's captain and bent over the sleeping officer. Then he put his sword to the captain's throat.

"Rock-a-bye baby," Ethan murmured in the man's ear. "It's almost dawn. Time to get up."

The captain opened one eye, and then the other. Through the shadows he saw with a shock a face he had never expected to see in his own bedroom. Squirming under Ethan's sword, he begged, "Spare my life, Allen. I'll give you the fort." He pointed to his sword on a nearby bench.

Ethan bowed and took the sword. He knew this meant that the fort was his.

Just then, there was a great shout in the yard. At this the captain jumped to his feet. "Now it's my turn, Ethan Allen! Those are my men gathering outside. You're trapped. I'll see you hanged before daylight for your pains!"

The captain marched to the window and looked out. But what he saw was not a gathering of British soldiers. It was the small army of Ethan Allen's Green Mountain Boys. He sank into a chair, unable to believe what had happened.

"I've lost my fort, my troops, my cannons," he moaned. "And all to a ragged band of mountain men!"

Ethan Allen went out to his men. They cheered when he held up the sword of surrender. "We've taken the fort!" he shouted. "We've taken it without firing a shot!"

The Green Mountain Boys threw their hats, still wet from the lake, high in the air. "We've won," they cheered. "Ticonderoga is ours!" And before many years had passed, so was the United States of America.

THE STRANGE ADVENTURE
OF RIP VAN WINKLE

Vocabulary Preview

demand   [*de MAND*]—ask for something very strongly
I *demand* an answer to my question.

nag   [*NAG*]—scold a lot
The man was tired of hearing his wife *nag* him all day.

peddler   [*PED ler*]—a person who carries things to sell
The *peddler* visited each town three times a year.

tremble   [*TREM bl*]—shake
Some people *tremble* when they hear thunder.

Bob looked at the clock on his friend's kitchen shelf. "What? Is it ten o'clock already?" he asked. "I promised to be home by nine! Wow! Time sure does fly!"

Do you remember times when the hours seemed to slip by almost before you knew they were gone? If so, you must have been very busy talking, reading or doing something else that you enjoyed.

Rip Van Winkle had a strange adventure with time. The story of what happened to Rip is one of Washington Irving's best-loved tales. Some people say it's a funny story. Others say it's a little bit sad and frightening.

After you read it, decide for yourself which group you think is right.

MANY YEARS AGO—more years than some people think—Rip Van Winkle lived in a village at the foot of the Catskill Mountains. It was an old village, settled by the Dutch at the time of Peter Stuyvesant. Now it belonged to England.

But this brought no great change to the quiet little town. Blue smoke still curled up from the chimneys. Old men still sat in the sun at the inn door and smoked their pipes. Young men worked in the fields as they always had. And the women took care of their neat, spotless homes. Things were as peaceful and quiet as they had been for a hundred years.

Things were quiet, that is, when Rip Van Winkle's wife wasn't screaming at her husband. One day Dame Van Winkle nagged so much that Rip ran right out of the house. He ran a whole mile before he stopped for a breath. Seeing how far he had come already, he decided to take a long walk to forget his troubles.

Soon Rip and his dog Wolf were out in the cool, green hills. "Peace and quiet at last," sighed Rip. "No noise, no nagging and no one to call me Turnip Head or Potato Brain! I could stay out here for years!"

As they were walking, Wolf spotted a squirrel. "Chase him up a tree, Wolf!" called Rip, running after them with his gun. "Hold him for the best hunter in these hills. And you know who that is!"

A voice called out, *"Rip Van Winkle!"*

"That's right!" laughed Rip. Then he stopped short. He stared hard at Wolf. "Did you say that?" he asked. Wolf only looked at Rip and barked. Rip shook his head. "I must have been hearing things," he told himself.

Then the voice called again. It sounded louder now: "RIP VAN WINKLE!" Slowly Rip looked up the nearby mountainside. There, standing on a rocky ledge was a short, square man with bright blue eyes and a long red beard. The man had a barrel on his back, and his clothes were very strange. They looked like the clothes worn by Dutch sailors over a hundred years before.

"Climb up here!" called the little man. "Help me with this barrel."

Rip was too surprised to say no.

"This way," ordered the small stranger. Then he began to climb the steep mountain. Rip followed over the rocky path, the barrel on his shoulders. The two climbed and climbed, higher and higher, until Rip didn't think he could take another step.

"Just a little farther, Rip Van Winkle," called the man.

"How does he know my name?" thought Rip. "I wonder who he is."

Just then the sound of thunder filled the air. Rip looked at the sky, but there were no clouds and no signs of rain. The noise grew louder and louder as they neared the mountaintop. When they reached the top, Rip saw what was causing it. On a flat, grassy spot near a tree, a dozen little men were playing nine-pins, a game like bowling.

One man seemed to be the captain. He had a long white beard and sharp gray eyes. His hat was too big for him, and he wore a long sword in his belt.

"Serve us the drink, Rip," he ordered. "Serve us the drink!" At once, Rip poured the contents of the barrel into cups the men held up.

"More!" the little men shouted. "More!" Rip busily filled their cups again and again. And again and again they demanded more. Finally, after more than an hour, the strange group went back to their game.

On and on they played. Rip sat down to watch. The oddest thing was that not one of the players ever smiled, even when all the pins were knocked down in one throw!

"How sad they look," thought Rip. He watched them until the moon came out. Then, growing thirsty, he poured himself a drink from the barrel. When he had emptied his cup, he began to feel very tired. After all, it had been a long and exciting day. He closed his eyes for a short rest.

As Rip slept, he dreamed of happy things. He dreamed that his wife couldn't speak above a whisper. He dreamed that he and Wolf had won a hunting contest. And he dreamed of his friends at the inn. He saw them talking and smoking their pipes. Rip had never had a more peaceful sleep.

Finally, he began to stretch and yawn. When he opened his eyes, he saw that the sun was high in the sky. "Why, I must have slept the whole night through," he exclaimed.

He got up hurriedly and called his dog. "Here, Wolf!

27

Time to go now." But Wolf was nowhere to be found. "He must have gone home last night," thought Rip. "*Home!* Oh dear, what will I tell my wife? She'll say that I talked to my friends at the inn all night. I'll never hear the end of it!"

Rip hurried down the steep path. Soon he was on the road to the village. He passed a few people on his way. They seemed to be staring at him. Then he looked down. Why, his clothes were old and torn! A white beard covered his chest!

Poor Rip ran the rest of the way. When he got to his house, he saw that it was in ruins. The windows were broken. The door was gone, and the roof had caved in. He didn't know what to think.

Rip turned and ran to the inn. A group of men were sitting outside the inn door. Rip ran up to them, but he saw at once that they were not his old friends. Who were these men? Where were his friends?

Then Rip looked up at the picture over the door. "Where's the picture of King George?" he cried. "Who is that strange man up there?" Rip read the name under the picture: "*George Washington*. Who is George Washington?"

A crowd began to gather around the old man. They stared at his ragged clothes and long beard. They shook their heads at his strange words.

"What's happening here?" Rip demanded. "I'm all confused. Just yesterday this was the King George Inn. I had a pint of ale right here at this table!"

"What's that?" said a man. "You must be mad. This hasn't been the King George Inn for twenty years! Don't you know there's been a war? Don't you know the colonies are free?"

Rip was more confused than ever. He didn't know what

was going on. And he didn't know any of the people standing around him. He wondered if they knew his name.

"Does no one here know Rip Van Winkle?" he cried.

"Oh, Rip Van Winkle," answered a girl. "Yes, we know him. That's Rip Van Winkle over there by the tree."

Rip turned. He saw a young man who looked just as Rip looked when he went up the mountain!

"I'm not myself," cried Rip. "I'm somebody else. That's me standing under the tree! No—that's somebody else with my face. I was myself last night, but I fell asleep on the mountain. Now everything is changed. I don't know what my name is or who I am!"

At that moment, a young lady pushed through the crowd. She carried a fat baby in her arms. Rip stared at her. He had a feeling that he knew her somehow.

"What's your name?" he asked.

"My name is Judith," answered the girl.

"And what's your father's name?" asked Rip.

"My poor father! Rip Van Winkle was his name," she said. "But it's twenty years since he went away from home. Perhaps he got lost in the mountains. Perhaps he was carried away by Indians. No one can tell. I was only a little girl then."

Rip asked one more question. "Where is your mother?"

"She died a short time ago," answered Judith. "She burst a blood vessel from screaming too long at a peddler."

Rip smiled broadly at the girl. "Then I'm your father!" he cried. "Don't you know me?"

The girl looked carefully into his eyes. Then, crying with joy, she ran to his arms. Rip danced around and around with his daughter, laughing and crying at the same time. Then Rip and the young man who looked like him hugged each other. No father and son ever looked more alike than did Rip and his son.

In a while, Rip sat down to tell his tale. He told about the little men and their powerful drink. And he told about his long sleep. But most of the people just laughed and tapped their foreheads.

Then a wise old man of the village pushed through the crowd. "I heard your story," he said. "And I believe every word of it." Everyone stopped laughing.

The old man went on, "My father told me of such things. He told me that when it thunders but doesn't rain, ghosts are playing nine-pins in the mountains. The ghosts are those of Henry Hudson and his crew."

Rip began to shake. "*Ghosts?*" he said. "Was I the guest of ghosts?" He rolled his eyes in terror.

After that, Rip became an important man in the town. He would sit before the inn, and people would come to hear him talk about the ghosts of Henry Hudson and his men. How Rip would make his listeners tremble!

One day, though, Rip tried to stretch the truth a bit. "The ghosts asked me to play nine-pins with them," he said. He was just about to say that he'd beaten Henry Hudson himself in a game. Then he heard a great clap of thunder roll out of the hills, and he held his tongue. On and on the thunder rolled. It made Rip think of his long, long sleep, and he was frightened.

After that, Rip Van Winkle always told his story *just as it really happened.*

THE HEADLESS HORSEMAN
OF SLEEPY HOLLOW

chatter   [*CHAT er*]—click together quickly
          The man's teeth began to *chatter* because he was so
          cold.
steeple   [*STEE pl*]—tall, pointed tower on the roof of a church
          The church *steeple* was taller than any other building
          in the small town.

Different parts of America are said to be haunted by different ghosts. South Carolina, for instance, has a special ghost of its own —the *plat-eye*. Whenever there is a full moon, this ghost is said to appear as a dog with fiery eyes. Anyone who stares into those eyes soon falls under the ghost's power.

About two miles from Tarrytown, New York, is a valley called Sleepy Hollow. This valley is believed to be haunted by many ghosts. One of them is the frightful Headless Horseman, the ghost of a man with no head on his shoulders, riding a great black horse.

Who is this ghost? Why does he ride about on horseback? Why is he headless? The answers to these questions will become clear when you visit Sleepy Hollow—or when you read this version of Washington Irving's famous story, "The Legend of Sleepy Hollow."

EVERYONE BELIEVED that the valley of Sleepy Hollow was haunted. But the one who believed it most was Ichabod Crane. Ichabod lived in Sleepy Hollow. And it was a good place for him, since he loved to read about goblins and witches and to tell frightening ghost stories.

Of course, Ichabod didn't spend all his time thinking about ghosts. He also thought about food. Even in school he thought about it. He would often lose his place in a book because his mind was on lunch instead of his work. This wouldn't have been so unusual, except that *Ichabod was the teacher!*

One afternoon, Ichabod gave his class a problem in arithmetic. Smacking his lips, he asked, "If you have six cakes, three cakes and ten cakes, how many cakes do you have?" The class set to work to find the answer. Ichabod walked

33

around with a stick in his hand to "help along" any pupil who seemed lazy.

As the class was working, a young man rode up to the schoolhouse door. "There's a party at the Van Tassel farm tonight," he called to Ichabod. "And you're invited. Supper is at eight o'clock."

"Wonderful!" answered the schoolmaster. "Thank you for the news!" He watched with excitement as the young man rode off to invite the other guests. Then Ichabod turned to his class.

"My dear children," he beamed. "Is your work finished?" He was so happy that he didn't even whip the boy who gave the wrong answer to the problem. In fact, he gave the class the rest of the day off.

Ichabod rushed home to get ready for the big night ahead. He hummed as he took a steaming hot bath, shined his best shoes and carefully brushed his Sunday suit. He spent half an hour just combing his hair. And as he stood in front of the mirror, he thought about Katrina.

Beautiful Katrina! She was the daughter of Mr. and Mrs. Van Tassel. How lovely she was, with her big brown eyes and shining curls. And how rich! If only she would marry him. Then they could sit at her parents' wonderful dinner table every single day!

Ichabod took a last look in the mirror. "What a handsome fellow!" he said to the face in the glass. Then he went to borrow a horse from the farmer in whose house he lived.

Soon Ichabod was bouncing up the road on the sagging back of old Gunpowder, Farmer Brown's gentlest horse. People smiled as the pair rode by. "Crane is certainly the right name for our good teacher," one man chuckled. "He looks just like that bird."

34

It was true. Ichabod had a long, skinny neck and long, skinny legs. His feet almost touched the ground as he rode. His pointed elbows stuck out on either side. They flapped up and down with Gunpowder's every step. Even the tails of Ichabod's coat fluttered behind him like a bird's tail feathers!

In a short while, Ichabod reached the Van Tassel farmhouse. Mr. Van Tassel met him at the door. "Welcome, Master Crane," said his host. "Come in and join the others."

Ichabod hurried inside, but he paid little attention to the other guests. He simply couldn't take his eyes off the food. Never had he seen such a table! When everyone sat down to dinner, he was the first to reach for the heaping bowls and platters. And each time his plate was empty, he was talked into having "just a bit more."

As everyone was eating, a noise like rolling thunder was heard outside. No one was afraid, though. They knew it was only young Brom Bones and his friends racing up the road on their horses. Katrina ran to the door with a blush. She waved shyly as Brom leaped off his horse.

Brom led his laughing friends into the house. They were jolly, handsome young men. Brom bowed to Mr. and Mrs. Van Tassel and winked at their pretty blond daughter. Then he went to shake hands with the guests.

In less than a minute, Brom was telling a funny story. It was about a trick he had played on a friend. The guests laughed until tears ran down their cheeks. They loved to hear Brom's merry tales.

One guest, however, didn't care for Brom's tales at all. Ichabod Crane only turned up his long nose at the storyteller and yawned. He was sure Katrina didn't like Brom Bones either. Certainly she had smiled at Brom just to be kind.

35

"After all," thought Ichabod, "Brom is just a joker. But I am a teacher! I've read three books all the way through. And I can sing like a bird." To prove it, he burst into song.

Ichabod's voice rang through the room like a great bell—a great bell with a great crack in it! People's eyes popped open in wonder at the noise. A few guests put their hands over their ears. But Ichabod thought they were only amazed at his wonderful talent.

Before long, someone began to play a fiddle. Ichabod didn't waste a moment. He was sure that he could dance as well as he could sing. And how right he was! Ichabod led Katrina to the middle of the floor and began to dance. His body shook from head to toe. His arms waved like flapping fans. He jumped from side to side and rolled his eyes. Katrina laughed as she tried to keep up. But Brom Bones wasn't laughing.

When the music stopped, Ichabod hurried to join some guests near the fire. They were telling ghost stories, and Ichabod dearly loved such tales.

"A strange woman in white appears in the graveyard just before each big storm," the blacksmith was saying. "I tell you, I've seen her twice!"

Ichabod's teeth began to chatter. Brom saw him and smiled. The mayor's wife went on. "I'm more afraid of the Headless Horseman."

"The Headless Horseman?" Ichabod asked in a weak voice. "What's that?"

Brom spoke up. "The Headless Horseman is the ghost of a soldier whose head was shot from his shoulders. Even now, the ghost sometimes rides through the night in search of his lost head."

Ichabod shook from head to foot. He believed every word of the story with all his heart.

Soon the party was over. Still shaking, Ichabod went to say good night to Katrina. However, she turned away, hardly noticing that he was there.

Poor Ichabod. Unhappily he started his trip home on Gunpowder. But as he rode through the dark night, a strange feeling came over him. "How foolish," he thought. "There are no ghosts out here. I know better than to believe in such things." Still, unhappy as he was, he couldn't get his mind off the tales he had heard—especially the one about the Headless Horseman.

Suddenly Ichabod felt a chill up and down his back. Now he really began to shake. He had a strong feeling that he wasn't alone. His heart pounding, he looked to the left and to the right. But he saw nothing unusual. Then he stared up the road in front of him. All he could see was the old church steeple, looking just the same as always. Still trembling, he rode on.

Ichabod came to a small wooden bridge. Gunpowder set one foot on it, then jerked to a sudden stop. Now Ichabod heard a step behind him. He sat up in his saddle. Drops of sweat stood out on his forehead. Slowly he turned his long neck to peek at the road behind him. Something big and black was standing in the darkness! It looked like a monster ready to spring!

Ichabod almost fainted. The monster was a huge horse and rider, not far behind. The teacher rubbed his eyes. Then he let out a wild scream!

"The Headless Horseman!" he cried. "The Headless Horseman is after me! Help! Somebody!" He dug his skinny heels into Gunpowder's ribs. The old farm horse gave a leap and began to gallop wildly down the road.

"Faster! Faster!" cried Ichabod, his long legs kicking in the air. He looked back to see if the Horseman had been left behind. But no, the awful thing was even closer!

Ichabod shook as if he would fall apart. His teeth chattered louder than Gunpowder's hoofs. He saw that the ghost *did* have a head—*but it was carrying its head under its arm!*

Now the Horseman started to swing its head around and around in the air. Higher and higher it swung it, faster and faster.

"No!" screamed Ichabod. "No! Don't do it!" He dug his heels deeper into Gunpowder's sweating sides.

The old horse did his best to pick up speed. Up steep hills and down deep valleys they raced. Sparks flew through the night as Gunpowder's hoofs hit the stones.

"Help! It's after me! It's after me!" Ichabod howled. He looked back once more and gasped. The terrible thing was only a few feet away!

Suddenly the Headless Horseman rushed forward. It swung its head high in the air. Then it let go! Ichabod tried to duck, but the head flew straight toward him! He screamed with all his might.

"*Y-A-A-A-a-a-a-a-a!*" he howled, as the head hit him squarely in the back and broke into pieces. Ichabod threw up his long arms and fell off Gunpowder's back in a heap. Down the hill he tumbled, head over heels. Then he jumped up. Still howling, he raced through the night, his arms waving as he went. Faster and faster he ran, farther and farther, until he was only a speck in the road.

From that night on, Ichabod Crane was never seen in Sleepy Hollow again.

The next morning, a very tired old Gunpowder was found eating grass at his master's front gate. The farmer wondered where Ichabod could be. So did the children who stood by the schoolhouse door waiting for their teacher. Many people looked for Ichabod, but he was not to be found. What *was* found were the tracks of horses' hoofs along the road from the Van Tassel farm. And not far from the tracks was a broken pumpkin.

One of the men in the search party told Brom Bones about the broken pumpkin. Brom burst out laughing as if he had just heard the best joke of his life. And for years after, even when he had been married to Katrina for a very long time, Brom would laugh for hours if someone just mentioned the word "pumpkin," or the name of Ichabod Crane.

JOHNNY APPLESEED'S SECRET

Vocabulary Preview

beast   [*BEEST*]—animal
The lion tamer wasn't afraid of the wild *beast*.

proverb   [*PRAH verb*]—a wise saying
"A penny saved is a penny earned" is an old *proverb*.

puzzled   [*PUZ zld*]—confused.
The story *puzzled* him because it didn't make sense.

reward   [*ree WARD*]—present or gift of money given in return for something
Tom was given a *reward* for finding the gold watch.

scout   [*SKOWT*]—person sent out for information
The army *scout* brought back news about the number of men in the enemy camp.

"As ye sow, so shall ye reap," says an old proverb. What does it mean?

The statement means that a person who sows, or plants, good seeds will reap, or harvest, good crops. But the person who plants poor seeds will get poor crops in return. A shorter way of saying it might be: "Good brings about good, and bad brings about bad."

When you do your school work properly, why are you "planting good seeds"? What "crops" might you expect to reap some day?

This story of "good seeds" is about John Chapman of Massachusetts—better known as Johnny Appleseed. According to the legend, Johnny Appleseed walked from Pennsylvania to Ohio and Indiana many times just to plant his apple seeds. He is said to have planted thousands of seeds during his travels, for he wanted Americans to enjoy the beauty and delicious fruit of the apple tree.

But John Chapman sowed more than just apple seeds. He sowed something that helped other people as well as himself. Read this story to find out what that important "something" was.

IT WAS A COOL, CLEAR EVENING in the summer of 1812. Hank and Tess Green stood at the door of their Ohio farmhouse. They were watching the moon and stars come out in the pale night sky. Suddenly they saw their son racing across the fields toward them. He was out of breath and very excited.

"What is it, James?" his mother called. "What's wrong?"

"There's a man in the south field," the boy answered, puffing to catch his breath. "His clothes are the strangest I've ever seen, and *he's talking to a horse!*"

43

"Oh, Jimmy, you're seeing things," laughed the boy's mother.

"That may be," said his father. "But I don't think we should take any chances. This is 1812, you know, and we are at war with England. Maybe James saw a scout for the English soldiers." He made his wife and son go into the house. Then he picked up his gun and went back to the doorway.

"There *is* a man out there," he said. "And he has a horse with him." Tess crept up to the door and peeked out. Then, before Hank could stop her, she ran out of the house!

Her husband ran after her. "Come back, Tessie!" he cried. "What are you doing?" But Tess ran right to the strange man and hugged him like a long-lost brother. Hank hurried down the road, puzzled by his wife's actions.

"Come on, Hank," Tess called to her husband. "It's all right. It's John Chapman!"

Hank stared at the man. Then a smile covered his face. "Why," he exclaimed, "Johnny Appleseed!"

Tess and Hank walked their old friend to the house. James saw that the odd-looking stranger was short and not very young. His shirt was just a sack with holes cut out for his head and arms. For a belt, he wore a rope around his waist. His hair was long and white, and an iron pot served as his hat. He walked barefoot. It was plain that Johnny Appleseed didn't care for fancy clothes.

Johnny shook hands with James. "You were only three years old when I saw you last," he said. "You must be twelve this year. What a tall young man you've become."

Hank smiled at his old friend. "It's good to see you after so many years, Johnny," he said. "The seeds you sowed here have grown into fine trees, rich with fruit."

44

Johnny's eyes twinkled. Nothing could have pleased him more.

"Tell me," said Tess, "do you have seeds with you now?"

Johnny held up a big sack. "Of course," he laughed. "I plant them wherever they'll grow. You know I've done it all my life."

"Yes," said Tess. "I know. But that's enough talking. Right now you must eat and rest. Come into the house and we'll have supper."

Johnny thanked Tess. "I'll be right there," he said. "Just let me water my horse first." He led the animal to a stream near the house. The poor beast hung his head and limped as he walked.

Hank watched the horse drink. "He looks sick to me," he said.

"He is sick," Johnny answered. "I saw a man beating him, so I bought him. But he's a good horse. All he needs is love and care to make him fit as a fiddle again."

Hank looked at the animal. "I sure could use a good horse," he sighed. "But we haven't a nickel to spare for one."

"In that case, the horse is yours!" exclaimed Johnny. "He needs a good home."

Hank tried to refuse, but Johnny wouldn't hear of it. "You're a kind man," he said. "You'll treat him well. The horse will have a good life for the first time. Knowing that is worth more to me than gold. It's all the payment I need!"

The men went into the house. There was food on the table. Soon everyone was eating and laughing, trying to catch up on the nine years that had passed. Hank asked Johnny if he had any news of the war. "You've walked from state to state planting seeds," Hank said. "You must have heard something."

Johnny frowned. "I can't lie to you," he said. "I do have news, for you and for everyone in this area. But trust me, Hank. Let me keep it a secret until morning."

Hank laughed. He said of course Johnny should do just as he pleased.

Morning came, and Tess prepared one of her biggest breakfasts. When they had all finished eating, Hank stood up and stretched.

"Think I'll have a look at the fields now," he said to his guest. Johnny looked at him seriously. "Wait," he said. "I think you'd better hear my news first."

The Greens turned toward Johnny. He went on, "Hank, I'm afraid you won't be able to work on the farm for a while."

Hank's eyes opened wide. "Not work on the farm?" he said. "But I have to work my land. The crops need care or they'll spoil. They're *my* life's work."

"I know. I'm glad you love growing things as I do," said Johnny. "But there are times when other things must come first. This is one of those times. Right now I'd like to be out planting too. But there's something else I must do instead."

The Greens didn't know what to think. "What is it you must do instead?" asked James.

"I must warn the settlers that the British are on their way here!"

"The British! But why didn't you tell us last night?" Hank asked.

"Because the soldiers and their Indian scouts won't arrive for a day or two. I came through the woods to get here. I'm way ahead of them."

46

Johnny stood up and picked up his bag of seeds. "You wouldn't have slept if you'd known this last night," he said. "Now you have your strength. Take your things and get over to the fort right away. You'll be safe there."

Hank thanked Johnny over and over and shook his hand warmly. "I can't believe it," he said. "You walked hundreds of miles just to warn us. You're the kindest man in the world!"

Johnny smiled and shook his head. "No, no!" he said. "It wasn't anything." He walked to the door and wished his friends good luck. Then, as the Greens stood watching him, he set out along the road to warn more settlers.

Suddenly James cried, "Look! There's a rattlesnake in his path! I don't think Johnny sees it!"

Hank warned his family not to shout. A sudden noise might cause the snake to strike. The family stood still, holding its breath. It watched the snake move slowly inch by inch toward Johnny's bare feet. He was walking straight toward it. He would probably step right on its head!

Then a strange thing happened! The rattlesnake came right up to Johnny—and stopped! Johnny looked down. He seemed to be talking to the snake. Then he walked on, whistling a tune as he went. The snake slid calmly back into the grass.

"Did you see that?" asked James. "The snake didn't touch him! Johnny has magic powers. I know he does! I told you he was talking to the horse!"

"He does have magic powers," said Tess. "It's a magic called kindness. It's very strong."

That same morning the Greens packed up their things and left the farm. They reached the fort by nightfall, along with the other settlers whom Johnny had been able to warn.

The Indian scouts came early the next day. But since they

found no one to fight at the Green farm, they left the house alone. They didn't even set fire to the crops. All they did was take a cool drink at the stream and help themselves to some food in the kitchen before riding on. Johnny's warning had saved his friends' farm and their lives. But—as everyone knows—the reward had been his as well as theirs.

JOE MAGARAC,
MYSTERY MAN OF STEEL

Vocabulary Preview

comet   [*KAHM it*]—fast-moving, star-like object in the sky often with a tail of light
The *comet* went speeding across the sky.

furnace   [*FER nes*]—large heater usually found in a factory or in the basement of a house
The worker put more coal on the fire in the large *furnace*.

molten   [*MOLE ten*]—melted into liquid by great heat
The *molten* steel was poured out of the great vat.

ore   [*OR*]—rocks or earth containing metal
The miner found some *ore* with gold in it.

scoop   [*SKOOP*]—dig out
Farmers *scoop* holes in the ground and plant seeds in them.

50

Every person has a special dream about his life and future. A boy may hope to become a pilot, a baseball star or a scientist. Or he may picture himself in a doctor's white jacket. A girl may dream about being a teacher, a model—or the first woman to land on the moon.

Joe Magarac had a very special dream. For, as you will see, he was a very special man. He held onto his dream for many years until he found the chance to make it come true. With it, best of all, came the chance to help his friends when they needed him most.

This story tells how it all happened.

I⟶T WAS A MORNING LIKE ANY OTHER in Pittsburgh, Pennsylvania. At exactly 8:07, all the buildings along Bessemer Street began to shake as if there were an earthquake. Leaves fell from the trees and windows rattled as a great THUMP, THUMP, THUMP was heard. Louder and louder the thumping grew, faster and faster. The very housetops seemed to come loose!

"That'll be Joe Magarac on his way to work," said Jim Janson to his wife Sarah. He picked up his teacup to keep it from falling off the table. "You could set your clock by him, that's sure."

The noise grew louder. Then, in a moment, the figure of a twenty-foot giant of a man swung around the corner.

"Don't worry, Pete," Joe called to his best friend, perched on his shoulder. "We'll get there on time!" Pete just laughed and held on for dear life to the scarf around Joe's neck.

Sarah Janson stopped her dishwashing to watch the pair speeding by. "Do you know what some folks say?" she asked her husband. "Some folks say Joe Magarac's a giant from inside the earth. I don't think so, though. I think he's from the stars."

"What do you mean, from the stars?" asked Jim. "Joe's just a plain man like anyone else. He can't help being so tall and strong. He just grew that way."

"*No* man just grows that way," Sarah insisted. "He looks as tough as steel. Some people even think he's *made* of steel!"

Jim shook his head at his wife's talk, but he couldn't change her mind. No one could change Sarah Janson's mind once she made it up.

"I say he came down from the stars," she said again, wiping her hands on her apron. "After all, I did see a comet in the sky that night last winter. It had a long, flaming orange and yellow tail. And on the very next day, Joe Magarac was seen in this town for the first time!"

Jim laughed. "What you saw was the glow of flames from the steel mill," he said. But it was no use talking to his wife. She was as sure she was right about this as she was about everything else.

Big Joe Magarac wasn't thinking about where he had come from, however. He was too busy racing toward the steel mill with Pete. As usual, they got to their furnace just as the morning whistle blew.

Joe looked down into the great vat of steel boiling in the furnace, and his eyes sparkled. He loved his work. Winking at Pete, he looked around to be sure they were alone. No one but Pete was allowed to see him at work.

Then Joe plunged his huge arm right into the molten steel! Singing, he stirred the liquid metal around and around. Finally

52

he scooped up a handful. Closing his fist, he squeezed the soft metal between his fingers. Out shot yards and yards of railroad track!

"They're perfect!" cried Pete. "Just perfect!"

Joe laughed and scooped up another handful of steel. This time he rolled it around his little finger to make dozens and dozens of train wheels. He pulled the rest of the metal out like taffy to make beams for new buildings.

Joe Magarac worked on and on. He did more work in an hour than twenty men could do in a day. And he was so happy that he sang as he worked.

But something was about to spoil Joe's happiness. When the day's work was over, the boss called the men together. He had bad news.

"Men," he said, "there will be no more work for at least a few days. All the iron ore in the mill has been used up. We'll have to wait until the railroads can bring in more."

Pete turned pale. He had been married for just a month. He still owed money for lots of things. The loss of even one day's pay would be hard for him.

"And I've got worse news than that," the boss went on. "Our biggest buyer needs more steel right now. If we can't give it to him within the next two days, he'll have to buy from another mill. If we lose this buyer, we might as well close up for good."

The men walked home with heavy hearts. How would they tell their families the bad news? Joe felt sorry for Pete and the others. He wished there was a way he could help.

That night, Joe couldn't eat or sleep. He walked and walked under the stars. Then, all at once, he snapped his fingers. He had thought of a way out. Joe turned and ran full speed toward the steel mill.

53

Pete and Mary were worried about Joe. They wondered why he hadn't come for supper as he usually did.

"Do you think he's sick?" asked Mary.

"No," answered Pete. "I think he's just sad about the bad news. I'll bet he's just sitting at home, thinking and worrying."

Mary put on her coat. "Come on," she said. "We're not going to let Joe stay home all alone on a night like this."

Pete and his wife walked quickly up the street. As they walked, Pete looked up at the sky. "Look!" he said. "There are orange and yellow lights all over the sky!"

Mary looked up. Then she looked toward the steel mill. "There!" she cried. "There's where the lights are coming from. Look how the windows are blazing!"

Now other people began to notice the lights from the steel mill. Some of the men started to run toward the mill.

"Be careful!" called their wives.

The men ran as fast as they could. Was the mill on fire? Had one of the furnaces blown up? What was happening?

When the men reached the mill, they found a great fire blazing in the largest furnace—Joe's furnace. Flames were shooting fifty feet into the air. Everyone but Pete ran to check the rest of the furnaces in the mill. They thought there might be more fires. Pete stayed because he thought he had heard a voice singing.

Pete climbed the high platform. Then he looked down into the vat of molten steel. The heat was awful! The bubbling steel was white hot and glowing as brightly as the sun.

Pete put his hands up to shade his eyes. Then he took a second look. "No!" he cried. "It can't be! Joe Magarac's in there!"

But it was true. Joe was inside the great vat. The bubbling steel was up to his waist.

"Joe, what are you doing?" shouted Pete. "Jump out before the steel burns you!"

"But all this steel is *me!*" laughed Joe. "I'm doing something I've wanted to do all my life."

Pete begged, "Please get out of there, Joe! I'll put out the fire in the furnace."

But nothing Pete said could make Joe Magarac change his mind. Soon the molten steel was up to his chest.

Joe's eyes flashed with joy as the bright drops of white-hot steel splashed around him. He was making his greatest dream come true. He was giving Pittsburgh the finest steel it had ever seen.

Pete ran for help. "Hurry," he cried to the men. "Joe's up there in the vat. Help me get him out!"

The men climbed the platform and looked down. But they didn't see Joe Magarac. What they saw was a huge vat of beautiful liquid steel. They looked at Pete and started to laugh. They were sure it was a joke.

Yet when the steel was poured out, it flashed and shone just like a comet's tail. It was the finest steel anyone had ever seen. That fine steel was made into many things—rails, wheels, spikes and beams. No one but Pete ever knew where it came from. And that steel, like the legend of mighty Joe Magarac, has lasted to this very day.

CLARA BARTON,
THE NURSE WHO
WON BATTLES

epidemic   [*ep eh* DEM *ik*]—widespread disease
Many people were given medicine to try to halt the *epidemic*.

international   [*in tur* NASH *uh nul*]—carried on between two or more nations
The family went to an *international* fair last year.

officials   [*uh* FISH *uls*]—people who hold public office or who are in charge
Senators and other *officials* were at the meeting.

organization   [*or guh neh* ZA *shun*]—society, club, or group of people united for a special purpose
The students formed an *organization* to fight pollution.

surgeon   [SIR *jun*]—doctor trained to perform operations
The chief *surgeon* at the hospital explained the difficult operation to the new doctors.

victims   [VIK *timz*]—hurt and suffering people or things
The *victims* of the flood were given food and shelter.

58

In this book you will find some stories about American women who were very courageous. Each of them was a fighter in her own way. For example, Harriet Tubman fought against injustice, and Sacajawea battled the forces of nature to help two explorers. Can you think of other women from the past or present who might be called real fighters?

This story is about Clara Barton who was born in Oxford, Massachusetts, on Christmas Day, 1821. Read to find out about this great person's special wish and how she fought to help make it come true.

CLARA BARTON'S BROWN EYES sparkled as she listened to her father's stories about his days as a fighter during the frontier wars. "I want to be a soldier, too!" the little girl shouted. This made everyone smile, for Clara was both very small and very shy. But her family couldn't imagine just how brave and strong this girl would prove to be in the years ahead.

One day, when Clara was eleven years old, the family was watching David Barton fix the barn roof. Suddenly he slipped, and the young man came spinning down through the air. He hit the ground with a loud thud.

Someone tried to hold Clara back. But she shouted, *"Let me go! Let me go!"* as she ran to David. She had always been frightened at the sight of blood, yet she was always able to forget her own problems when someone else needed her help.

During the months that followed, the young girl worked hard to help her brother get well. Her parents and the doctors were amazed at her natural gift for nursing.

Later on, when she was a young woman, Clara became a teacher. Then she went to Washington, D.C., where she worked as the first woman clerk in the Patent Office.

When the Civil War broke out in 1861, Clara quit her clerkship and went to work as a volunteer nurse in army hospitals. One afternoon, Clara talked to a friend, an army surgeon. "I'd like to serve as a nurse on the battlefield," she said. He told her that the War Department wouldn't allow it.

"But soldiers need help right on the battlefield," Clara argued. "Many of them die before doctors can get to them. I only want to help these suffering men get better care."

The surgeon said the War Department would never give her a battlefield pass. Upon hearing this, Clara rushed over to the War Department. Her hoop skirt swished as she hurried from office to office. "Give me a special pass," she pleaded. *"Let me go! Let me go!"* But not one of the officials would give her the precious pass.

Still determined to help, Clara continued a job she had begun earlier. She collected food, blankets, and other supplies from generous people. Then she brought these things to hospitals to help the wounded men. But she never stopped hoping to help troops right on the battlefields.

Then one morning something wonderful happened. No one knows just who helped her, but Clara received an envelope containing a special pass. Soon after, she left for the dangerous battlefield with a few helpers and a wagon filled with supplies. And as Clara went along she helped any soldier, Northerner or Southerner, who needed care. Bullets went whistling by as Clara bandaged wounds, covered freezing men with blankets, and gave out food and drink to the troops.

One evening, one of the wounded troops called to her.

"Mary!" he cried. "My sister! I knew you'd come to help me."

Clara knelt in the mud and held the dying soldier in her arms. For hours she spoke to him as though she were his sister. Her tender care kept him alive until a doctor arrived.

Clara stood up and looked around at all the suffering men. She thought her heart would break. "Oh," she sighed, "how I wish there were some way to give suffering people more help." Just then a bullet tore through her sleeve, but she was unharmed. Clara remained very calm. She just brushed off her long skirt and said, "Let me go! Let me go!" as she hurried away to help more soldiers.

During one great battle, Clara went over to a red-haired soldier. She almost fainted when he looked up at her. "Please, Miss Barton," he begged. "Cut this bullet out of my face. I can't take the pain much longer."

Clara told him that a doctor should do that. But the soldier began to shake with pain. "Please, help me!" he almost screamed.

The little nurse was trembling. She opened a pocketknife, took a deep breath, and began digging into the flesh in the young man's face. Soon her hands were filled with blood— but she also had the bullet in her hand.

"Thank you," the soldier sobbed as he sank back to rest. Clara smiled as he fell asleep. Then she dressed the wound and went off to wash her hands. She had to get on with her job of preparing food for the hungry men.

Day after day, the courageous Clara Barton did her best to take care of wounds and to feed the weary soldiers. But on one day, after a terrible battle had been fought, she sat down and nearly cried. She found that she'd run out of food for the soldiers.

"We have only three cases left," she told a helper. "And they are cases of wine. The men will starve." Clara tried not to look at the sad-eyed men who were beginning to take seats around the campfire. Finally, Clara said, "Open the cases. At least the men will have wine."

But Clara's sadness soon turned to joy. She discovered that the bottles of wine had been shipped in crates filled with cornmeal. The little nurse laughed happily, and soon she was stirring kettles of hot cornmeal for the hungry men.

Clara kept on working hard all through the long war years. In 1864 she was put in charge of a group of hospitals at the front. When the war ended in 1865, President Lincoln put her in charge of the search for missing soldiers.

In 1870 a terrible war was fought in Europe called the Franco-Prussian War. Clara was hired to organize military hospitals. In 1871 she was put in charge of distributing work to the poor of Strasbourg. In 1872 she did similar work in Paris. When the war was over she received the Iron Cross of Merit of Prussia and the Gold Cross of Remembrance of Baden, Germany.

In Europe, Clara Barton saw the valuable work that the Red Cross did in caring for the wounded and suffering in time of war. When she came back to the United States she tried to get the government to approve of an American Red Cross. But many government officials didn't like the idea. One senator waved his arms and roared, "We don't need to sign that (Red Cross) treaty because America is finished with war!"

Clara stood her ground like a soldier. "Well," she argued, "then why don't we start an American Red Cross that will help people even in peacetime? We could help victims of hurricanes, floods, and other natural disasters."

Even this great idea didn't get the men in Washington to approve the treaty. However, this didn't stop the little fighter. When Clara went back to her home in Dansville, New York, she and the wonderful people there started their own local chapter of the Red Cross. And it was a good thing they had done this, for soon great forest fires broke out in the state of Michigan.

"We've got to help those people," Clara cried to her towns-people. "Thousands of people have been burned to death, and many thousands more are homeless."

At that moment a man rushed into the room. "Good news!" he shouted. "The people of Syracuse and Rochester have sent us money to help us in our work."

Everyone shouted for joy. And soon money, supplies, and volunteers were on their way in this mission of mercy.

Many newspapers printed stories about how Clara Barton's Red Cross had helped the people of Michigan. Soon people all over the land wanted to start local chapters of the Red Cross in their towns and cities. Word of this quickly reached Washington, and not long after that the President signed the treaty that set up rules for the Inernational Red Cross.

Clara Barton was honored by being made the first president of the American Red Cross. Through the years, Clara and her workers helped many victims of floods, hurricanes, earthquakes, fires, railroad accidents, epidemics, and other disasters. And this great work is still going on today.

The remarkable person who founded the American Red Cross lived to be ninety-one years old. She died on April 12, 1912, in Glen Echo, Maryland. People wondered what she might have been thinking about in her last moments. Was she thinking about her brother David's fall from the barn roof?

Was she thinking about helping soldiers on the battlefields? Was she thinking about helping victims of some great disaster? Or was she just thinking about finding peace and rest after years of struggling to help others? We will never know what was on the mind of this great lady. All we know is that as she took her last breath, she sat up once again and cried, *"Let me go! Let me go!"*

BOWLEG BILL, COWBOY
OF THE OCEAN WAVES

Vocabulary Preview

calm   [*KAHM*]—quiet and still
The winds were *calm*.

mackerel   [*MAK uh rel*]—kind of fish found in the ocean
The blue *mackerel* has dark stripes on its back.

pilot   [*PI lut*]—person who steers ships or flies planes
The *pilot* steers the big ship into the harbor.

reins   [*RAYNZ*]—leather straps used to drive horses
The man pulled up on the *reins* to make the horse stop running.

tuna   [*TOO nuh*]—large fish in the mackerel family
Some people enjoy a *tuna* sandwich for lunch.

whoop   [*HWOOP*]—yell, like the sound of an Indian battle cry
He let out a *whoop* as he chased after the buffalo.

Do you know the famous cry of the wagon-train leaders of the 1800's? These brave pioneers set out to find new homes and new adventures in the West. As they started out on their long, dangerous trips, they would cry, *Westward Ho!*

But have you ever heard the cry, *Eastward Ho?* Probably not. Yet these words would fit the legend of a man who traveled not from the East to the West, but from the West to the East.

What made this fearless cowboy go rushing East? What new adventures did he think he would find? And why might it be said that Bowleg Bill brought a lot of the Old West along with him? You'll find the answers to these questions by riding East with Bill in this story. So, *Eastward Ho!*

BOWLEG BILL'S EYES almost popped out of his head. "You say that you saw the Atlantic Ocean, Cliff, and it's *bigger* than the Great Plains?" Bill pushed back his twenty-gallon hat and scratched his head.

Colorado Cliff was one of Bill's best pals. He had just come back from a visit to his sister in Boston. "That's right," said Cliff. "I saw the ocean with my own eyes, and it's true."

Bill shook his head. "Mashed potatoes and black-eyed beans! I can't believe it. I'll have to see this ocean for myself."

Bill didn't waste any time. He leaped at once onto the back of his pet wild buffalo. (Horses were too small and slow for a man like Bill.) With a whoop and a holler, he started off East to see the great Atlantic.

Bill galloped all day Monday through Nebraska. Tuesday and Wednesday took him through Iowa and Illinois. "Hm," he thought as he rode along, "things are getting pretty crowded in these parts. Call me a puppy dog if the houses are more than five miles apart."

Soon Bill came to Lake Michigan and Lake Erie. He splashed across both in a morning and an afternoon. Then he crossed New York into Massachusetts. Finally he found himself in Boston. Leaving his buffalo to graze on the Boston Common, Bill set out to find the sea.

He stopped a stranger on the street. "Howdy, partner," he said. "Where might a body have a look at the ocean that's supposed to be around here?"

The stranger just stared at Bill's long hair and odd clothes. He had never seen a cowboy before. Finally he gulped, spun around and ran off down the street. Bill's jaw dropped. "These Eastern folk sure have a funny way of being friendly," he thought.

Then a small boy walked up to Bill. Of course, all young boys know a cowboy when they see one. "Hello, cowboy," he said. "I heard you asking where you could find the ocean. If you walk straight ahead for twenty or thirty yards, you'll fall right into it."

"Mashed potatoes and black-eyed beans!" laughed Bill. "So that's the Atlantic Ocean! I thank you kindly, son."

Bill hurried down to the edge of the dock. When he got there he just stood with his eyes opened wide. He was admiring the big boat that was swinging into the harbor. (He knew it was a boat because he'd seen a picture of one in a book back home.)

As Bill stood looking at the ship, the sky suddenly filled with stars. "Night sure falls fast in the East," he thought. With that, he fell flat on the dock.

It wasn't night, however, and Bill hadn't tripped. He had been hit over the head by kidnapers! The captain of the

68

big ship needed sailors, and he had hired the kidnapers to find him some. He wasn't choosy about where they found them, or how.

When Bill woke up an hour later, the sun was shining brightly. "I just can't get used to this," he said. "Nights and days follow each other too fast around here for me."

He stood up and tried to walk away. But to his surprise, the ground wouldn't stand still under his feet. Looking around, Bill saw that he was on the big boat—and that it was heading out to sea!

"Whoa," cried Bill, looking around for the boat's reins. He had never been on a boat before, and he thought it handled like a horse. Bill ran around pulling down on this rope and up on that, trying to stop the ship. But this only made the sails fly crazily up and down. Soon the ropes were all tangled.

"What's going on?" roared a voice from the top deck. "Why are we starboard when we should be larboard? Aft the mizzen and man the jib. Port, I say, port!" The captain stomped out of his cabin.

"Hey you, the new man!" he yelled. "Leave those ropes alone and get down to help the cook."

Bill put his hands on his hips and raised one eyebrow. "You talking to me, sonny?" he asked.

"Don't you call me *sonny!*" shouted the captain. "I'm the skipper on this ship, and don't you forget it."

Bill pulled out his guns. "That suits me fine," he said. "If you're the skipper, let's see you skip." And Bill began shooting at the captain's toes.

"YOW!" screamed the captain. He had to do some fancy jumping to keep his toes from being shot off. He skipped and danced and hopped and pranced as Bill fired shot after

69

shot. All around the ship they went, while the sailors roared with laughter. Not one of them lifted a finger to help their captain. He was the meanest, nastiest man who ever sailed out of Boston Harbor. They were glad to see him in trouble for a change.

But their fun was soon over. All at once the first mate pointed out to sea and cried, "Look, out there! Now we're in for it!"

Everyone ran to the rail. "Oh, no!" cried the captain. "It's the giant tuna!" He quickly forgot about his trouble with Bill. The giant tuna was a much bigger problem than the cowboy.

Bill was the only man who wasn't frightened. His eyes lit up with pleasure to see the giant fish leaping over the waves. It reminded him of the horses running wild and free in the hills of Wyoming.

The captain had reason to be worried. "We may never get this ship to England," he told Bill. "I forgot to take along a barrel of tea."

"A barrel of *tea?*" asked Bill. "What in tarnation has *tea* got to do with a big fish?"

"Every captain sailing in or out of Boston carries a barrel of tea," said the captain. "They do it just in case they meet that fish. That tuna's great-granddaddy got his first taste of tea during the Boston Tea Party in 1773. And this tuna has its great-granddaddy's taste for tea. I pity the captain and crew that don't have a barrel to throw over the side when that fish starts swimming in circles. Why, it could crash right into one side of this boat and out the other. And that would mean the end of us."

"Not a bad story," Bill snorted. "Tell me another." He laughed until the tears ran down his cheeks.

The rest of the crew didn't think it was so funny. They watched the monster fish's every move. They were hoping it would swim past their ship. But instead, it began to swim in circles!

Things looked pretty dark for the men on board. Even the captain had given up. "We're lost," he sighed. "That horse mackerel will tear a hole right through this ship and sink us all."

"*Horse?*" asked Bill, his eyes sparkling. "Did you say *horse?* Now I know what's been running through my mind ever since I saw that fish. I'd like to take me a ride on that horse whatever-you-call-it."

"But horse mackerel is just another name for a big tuna," said a sailor.

"Maybe so," answered Bill. "But it acts just like a horse, leaping around like that. And if it acts anything like a horse, I can ride it!"

The men still rushed to get the lifeboats. But meanwhile, Bill climbed up on the ship's rail. He waited until the tuna was just a few yards from the boat. Then he leaped!

The giant fish felt something happen, but it didn't know what. It didn't have to wait long to find out. Bill threw his belt around the huge fish's middle and held on tight. Now the tuna knew Bill meant to ride it.

It began speeding over the water. It flipped and flopped. It leaped and splashed. It threw itself into the air, twisting and turning with all its might. But it couldn't shake Bill off.

The angry tuna swam down deep into the ocean and then sailed up through the waves. It slapped and crashed over the water. It spun wildly into the air, higher and higher. It beat the sea so much that the water for miles around looked like whipped cream.

Then, just as the fish leaped over the ship, Bill started to sing:

"Yip-yip yippee! I'll steer the course
For buffalo, fish or the wildest horse.
There's not an animal I can't tame,
Or Bowleg Bill is not my name!"

And suddenly, like the quiet after a great storm, the sea was calm. The big horse mackerel floated gently on the waves. It swam slowly through the blue water, listening to Bill's songs.

The men couldn't believe their eyes! Not only had Bill "broken" the tuna—he'd taught it to like cowboy music!

Bill and the monster tuna got along so well that it carried him all the way back to Boston. They went riding together every day after that. Finally, Bill got so fond of his pet and of the ocean that he decided to stay in the East for good. After all, the Atlantic Ocean *was* bigger than the Great Plains.

Soon Bill found work as a pilot in Boston Harbor. It was his job to ride on the back of his horse mackerel and guide the big ships in and out of the harbor.

People soon got used to seeing Bowleg Bill and his horse mackerel ride by. And they were very proud of him. Whenever a stranger asked about Bill, they would say that the best pilot they had ever had was the singing cowboy from Wyoming.

PAUL BUNYAN AND HIS WONDERFUL BLUE OX

Vocabulary Preview

accounts   [*uh KOWNTS*]—records of money taken in and paid out
The child used to eat well, but now her *appetite* is poor.

Mr. Jones keeps the *accounts* for his company.

appetite   [*AP a tite*]—desire for food
The child used to eat well, but now her *appetite* is poor.

canoe   [*kuh NOO*]—small, narrow boat used on streams and lakes
The *canoe* tipped over in the bad storm.

earthquake   [*ERTH kwake*]—shaking of the earth
The *earthquake* caused damage to many houses.

lumberjack   [*LUM ber jak*]—man who cuts down trees
The *lumberjack* may use an ax or a saw for his work of felling trees.

nostrils   [*NAHS trilz*]—openings in the nose
The man put a handkerchief over his *nostrils* to keep out the dust from the road.

quiver   [*KWIV er*]—shake or shiver
When the little boy heard the thunder, his legs began to *quiver*.

slope   [*SLOPE*]—land that is on a slant, like the side of a hill
Great rocks tumbled down the *slope*.

74

When people see you carrying pencils and books, they know right away that you are a student. They know this because they can see that you are carrying the "tools of your trade."

What tools of the trade does each of the following people carry?

      A waiter in a restaurant
      A mailman
      A lumberjack

Suppose you saw some men carrying a canoe and some snow shovels. Would you think that these men were cooks? Well, Paul Bunyan's cooks used a canoe and snow shovels to help them prepare food. After reading this tale, you can decide for yourself whether the cooks really needed these things in their kitchen.

"IF ONLY PAUL BUNYAN were here now!" sighed Johnny Inkslinger. "He would save us from the storm."

Poor Johnny! He and the other men at Big Pine Camp were in real trouble. An hour before, it had started to snow. Now, the snowstorms in Maine are not like snowstorms anywhere else in the world. When it snows in Maine, it snows so fast and so hard that whole towns can be covered up before you can say "Jack Frost." And this was the worst snowstorm Johnny Inkslinger had ever seen.

As soon as it had started to snow, he and the other men of Big Pine Camp had climbed the tallest trees they could find. But the snow was piling higher and higher every minute. If it kept up much longer, they'd all be buried alive! "If only Paul Bunyan were here," Johnny wished.

Johnny Inkslinger was the man who kept the accounts for

Paul's camp. He was a small man, but he worked as hard as any lumberjack there. His office was filled from top to bottom with books of figures. And he used up twelve barrels of ink a day!

Everything in Johnny's office was blue—the floors, the desk, the chairs, the walls, even Johnny's hair. This was because he worked so hard and so fast that the ink flew all over everything. When he was working, he thought only of the numbers in front of him.

Everyone liked Johnny, for he was very kind. On his own time, he would write letters for the men. And he always had a friendly word or a joke for anyone who came by.

But he didn't feel like joking now, huddled on the branch of a tree. The snow was more than fifty feet deep already. Soon it would reach the tops of the trees. And he hadn't even had time to put on his coat.

Johnny shivered and looked around. As he did so, he saw a hole in the trunk of his tree. There was a big hollow place inside. Shaking with cold, he crawled into the hole to keep warm.

Johnny and the men didn't know it, but Paul Bunyan wasn't far away. The huge lumberjack had been off visiting his other lumber camps. He had camps from Maine to California. But now he was on his way back to his home camp in the East.

Paul walked along, taking small steps because he was in no great hurry. Of course, a small step for Paul was about three city blocks.

"Brrr, it's getting cold," he said as he pulled up the collar of his wool shirt. (It had taken a good many blankets sewn together to make that shirt.) Then, looking ahead into the distance, he saw the swirling snowstorm over his camp. But he had no idea of what was happening to his men.

Babe, Paul's blue ox, walked along beside him. Babe weighed fifteen tons before breakfast and stood sixty feet tall. From the tip of one horn to the tip of the other, she measured forty-six ax handles. Babe saw the snow too. She loved snow and began to run toward the storm.

"Whoa, Babe," laughed Paul. "If you run like that, people will think there's an earthquake."

Babe slowed to a walk, but she wasn't too happy. She wanted to get back to camp and slide down the big hill near the river. Paul knew what she was thinking and started to laugh again. He loved his big pet, and he wouldn't have parted with her for all the forests in the world. He put his arm across Babe's broad, blue back as they walked along.

Of course, Babe hadn't always been blue. But nobody knew for sure how she had come to be that color. Some said she had turned blue from playing outdoors too long during the Winter of the Blue Snow. Others claimed she was blue because she had once taken a nap right outside Johnny Ink- slinger's open window. In any case, Babe was a blue ox now, and Paul liked her that way.

As Babe and Paul got closer to camp, they saw the men perched like birds on the top branches of the trees. The snow was nearly eighty feet deep now. "Ha!" cried Paul. "It's a good thing we don't have *big* snowfalls like the ones when I was a boy! If this were a *real* snowstorm, the trees would have been covered up long ago."

Paul walked through the camp. He went from tree to tree, picking his men off the branches like so many apples. Then he put them into his pockets to warm up.

"The cooks!" Paul cried suddenly. "My men have the world's biggest appetites! They'll never forgive me if I don't rescue the cooks!"

Paul set to work and tunneled down through the snow. Finally he found his buried kitchen. He opened a window and peeped inside. The cooks were so busy that they barely looked up. Snowstorm or no snowstorm, there was always cooking to be done.

"Aren't you boys scared, buried under all this snow?" asked Paul.

"Not us," said Sourdough Sam, the chief cook. "We knew you'd save us somehow. Paul Bunyan's men never worry!"

Paul had a lot of work to do. But he stayed to watch the cooks for a while, just to see how things were going. First he looked into the soup kettle. It was fifty feet across at the top, and the soup in it was the size of a small lake. In fact, the way Soupy Sim stirred the soup was to paddle around the kettle in a canoe. From time to time he would drop in a bushel or two of vegetables.

The griddle for cooking pancakes and hamburgers was eighty feet wide. It smoked and hissed. Twenty-one cooks with bacon tied to their feet skated around on it to keep it greased up. The pancakes and hamburgers were so big that the cooks had to use snow shovels to flip them over.

Paul liked to watch the cooks work. He wanted to stay longer, but he had a busy day ahead. Snow or no snow, Paul had to send ten thousand logs down the river to the mill that day.

But the trees were buried under the snow. How was he going to reach them? He thought and thought, for Paul was a thinking man. Then he took the men out of his pockets and told them what had to be done.

"Men," he said, "get some shovels. Then dig until you find the tops of the trees. Babe and I will take care of the rest."

The men got busy right away. They dug all around the camp to find the trees. From time to time, a lumberjack would call, "Here's one!" Then Paul would run over and put one end of a long chain around the tree. The other end was wrapped around Babe's strong shoulders. Babe would tug and pull, and the tree would fly out of the snow like a rabbit out of a hole.

Babe and the men worked on for an hour or so. Soon they had ten thousand trees piled up on the big hill next to the frozen river.

"Hm," said Paul. "Even the weight of ten thousand logs won't break through ice that thick. There's only one thing to do."

Paul looked at Babe, and Babe knew right away what he was thinking. With a happy twinkle in her eye, she hopped up and landed on the steep slope. Slipping and sliding, she flew down the hillside.

"Whoopee!" cried the men as they watched Babe zoom down the hill. SPLASH! Babe hit the ice and broke it. Ice flew so high that it fell from the sky in nearby states for two days.

Now the river was free of ice, and the logs were sent rolling down the hill. They hit the water with a great crash. Soon they were floating swiftly toward the mill.

The men cheered and swung their shovels in the air. They were glad that even the big snow had not stopped them from getting their day's work done. They laughed and talked as they walked toward the dining hall for supper.

The men found their seats at the long dinner table. They were in a good mood, so they started to sing and bang on the table with their knives and forks. Paul stuck his head into the kitchen to see if supper was ready. As he looked around, he saw the list of things Sourdough Sam had used for the meal. It looked like this:

List for Tuesday Night's Supper
2 herds of cattle for steaks and hamburgers
1,000 barrels of flour for pancakes
200 gallons of maple syrup
500 gallons of milk
100 pounds of coffee
2,000 bushels of vegetables for soup
5,000 bushels of apples for pie
1 fresh rattlesnake

The rattlesnake was for Johnny Inkslinger. He liked nothing better than a good rattlesnake stew. Smiling, Paul picked up the bowl of stew for Johnny. He carried it over to the table. But when he reached the table, his mouth dropped open in surprise. Johnny had always been the first one to the table, but now his chair was empty!

"Where's Johnny?" Paul called out.

The men stopped singing. They looked toward Johnny's empty chair. Then they looked at each other and shook their heads. No one could think where Johnny might be. There was a long silence.

Suddenly a lumberjack slammed his big fist down on the table. "Now I remember!" he said. "The last time I saw Johnny, he was sitting up in that tree."

"What's that?" cried Paul. "I don't remember picking Johnny out of any tree. In fact, I don't remember seeing him at all today."

"That's just it," said the lumberjack. "You *didn't* see him, because he had crawled into a hole in the tree to keep warm!"

There was a silence. Everyone was thinking the same thing: *Johnny was in one of the logs rushing down the river!*

"Those logs are heading toward the big waterfall," said one man at last. "There's no way to save him!"

Scratching his big black beard, Paul thought as hard as he could.

"Not even Paul can think of a way to stop Johnny from going over the falls," moaned the men. "And Paul is a thinking man!"

But suddenly Paul stopped scratching his beard. He pulled out the grandfather clock he always carried around in his shirt pocket. "Those logs couldn't have reached the big falls yet," he said. "I think we've just got time."

Paul ran out to Babe and told her what she had to do. Babe's eyes opened wide. Then she ran to the river's edge. All the men, even the cooks in their white aprons, ran after her. What was Babe going to do? Was she going to swim after the logs? Big as she was, she could never make it in time.

Paul crossed his fingers. He hoped his idea would work. He watched Babe take a deep, deep breath. Then she stuck her nose into the water and began to drink.

"This is no time to stop for a drink!" cried one of the men. But Babe paid no attention. She just went on drinking, and drinking, and drinking.

The men could hardly believe their eyes! *Babe was drinking up the river!* The men could see the water in the river getting lower and lower. Soon all that was left was the muddy river bed. Hundreds of frogs sat in the mud, looking around and wondering where all the water had gone.

The men felt better now. They knew that down the river, somewhere, the logs had stopped moving. But Paul didn't waste any time. He started to run along the river bed, splashing through the mud. The men cheered him on until he was out of sight. Then they went back to the dining hall to wait for his return.

The men waited and waited. Each minute seemed like an hour. Ten minutes, then twenty, went by. Where was Paul? Had he found Johnny? Was their friend all right?

All at once the door swung open, and in walked Paul. But Johnny was nowhere in sight. The men groaned.

Paul made a sign for everyone to be quiet. Reaching into his pocket he pulled out the sleeping Johnny. "He was sound asleep when I found him, and he's still asleep," said Paul. The little bookkeeper snored as Paul set him down in his chair by the table.

Then Sourdough Sam held the dish of hot rattlesnake stew under Johnny's nose. Johnny's nostrils began to quiver. Then his eyebrows began to twitch. All at once his eyes flew open. He grabbed a spoon, and without even a "how do you do," he started to eat his favorite dish. The men all tried to ask him questions about his adventure, but Johnny just said, "Later! We'll talk later! Right now there's something more important to do." Then he shoved another steaming spoonful of stew into his mouth.

Now the men were happy again. They began to shout, "Bring on the food! Bring on the food!" Soon the tabletop was crowded with waiters rushing back and forth on rollerskates. It was the only way they could keep the milk glasses, coffee cups and bread baskets filled. Other waiters on bicycles rode around the long table with huge platters of steaks, hamburgers, pancakes and apple pie. The men ate and laughed and talked.

Babe had a good time too. As a reward for her wonderful

work, her dinner was three wagonloads of sweet potatoes and, for dessert, a fifty-foot hill of apples. She ate all of it, except for one apple. Remember, she was an ox, not a hog!

As for the river, a few puffs from Paul's after-dinner pipe were enough to melt some of the snow and send it streaming down to the riverbanks. A short time later, 9,999 logs floated into the mill. Paul had taken out the hollow one he had found Johnny in. After all, he didn't want the mill owner to think he was being cheated!

A GRAB BAG OF TALL
TALES *From the East*

In Wisconsin it sometimes gets so cold that the sunlight freezes on the ground. When this happens, the people don't use electric lights because they have the frozen sunlight to see by.

Once it was so cold in New Jersey that people's words froze right in the air while they were speaking. The people had to put all the words in a basket and thaw them out near a roaring fire to find out what their friends had said.

The fog in upstate New York was thicker than ever one night. But this didn't stop a man who was nailing shingles to the roof of his barn. He kept right on working until he ran out of shingles. When the fog lifted, he found that he'd shingled twelve feet beyond the roof of the barn.

In Pennsylvania there was an oil derrick so tall that the workers had to put the top on hinges just to let the moon pass by.

The people in Connecticut tell this story to explain why the trout in their state are rainbow-colored. They say that the Housatonic [*HOO sa TON ik*] River, famous for bass,

85

once held a bass so big that it swallowed the anchor a fisherman had thrown out. When the man tried to pull the anchor back in, the fish became very angry. It began swimming so fast that the water in the river boiled. The boiling water melted the paint off the man's boat, and all the colors ran into the river. Since that day there have been rainbow trout in Connecticut's waters.

A farmer in Rhode Island claimed to have hens that were so smart that they knew enough to lay chocolate eggs for Easter morning.

Old Chippewa (or Ojibwa) legends tell about Iagoo, an Indian who was one of the greatest braggers (and liars) of all time. Iagoo's own "fish story" is about the time he was annoyed by the quacking of ducks on the stream outside his lodge. It seems that he fired *without looking* through the door and killed a swan, forty ducks, two loons, and a giant fish that lived in the stream! Another of these tales tells of how Iagoo claimed to have seen giant mosquitoes. They were so large that one of their wings would have made a perfect sail for his canoe.

Heading South

THE FOUNTAIN
OF YOUTH

Vocabulary Preview

explorer [*eks PLOR er*]—a person who travels to find new lands
Christopher Columbus was a great *explorer*.

message [*MES ij*]—a letter or note containing information
John received a *message* from his uncle.

swoop [*SWOOP*]—to move smoothly and quickly down
We saw the birds *swoop* down to the ground.

tangles [*TANG glz*]—twists, windings
It took Jim a long time to unwind the *tangles* of string.

Try to imagine this scene. A friend who has always been very honest comes up to you with exciting news. "I always used to fail spelling tests, until one day I took a drink from a fountain in the park," he says. "I happened to have my spelling book under my arm, and now I pass all my tests. I think there's magic water in that fountain."

When you are through laughing, your friend goes on. "Just last week I took another drink from that fountain. This time I had my arithmetic book under my arm. Since that day I've passed all my arithmetic tests with perfect scores!"

What would you think then?

Perhaps now you can imagine the excitement of the men who set out to search for the Fountain of Youth. But you would be wrong if you thought all those who searched for it were old men who wanted to become young again. Read this story of what might have happened on that journey, and you will know another reason some of the men had for wanting to find the magic waters.

"A MESSAGE FROM THE KING! A message from the King!" cried the young sailor, waving a letter in the air. He had run all the way from his ship to the home of Juan Ponce de Leon [*HWAN PON the day lay ON*], Spanish governor of Puerto Rico.

Ponce took the letter and read it carefully. It said that the King of Spain was sending someone else to rule Puerto Rico. This, the letter said, was because the King wanted Ponce to lead a search for the famous Fountain of Youth. The fountain was supposed to be somewhere in the New World, but no one had ever seen it.

91

Ponce's eyes gleamed. "At last I can search for the magic fountain!" he exclaimed. The famous explorer already had many white hairs. He had wanted to find the Fountain of Youth for a long, long time.

Ponce and his crew prepared to sail. "We'll find the Fountain of Youth and drink from it," he told his men happily. "And then we'll all go back to Puerto Rico as young men!"

The older sailors cheered, for they wanted very much to be young again. The young sailors cheered too, but they had other reasons. They were thinking of how rich they would become by selling the magic water to old people all over the world.

Ponce and his men sailed for weeks and weeks. They searched the many islands around Puerto Rico. They sailed to places where they had never been before. But after long months of searching, they began to get restless. Some of them wanted to turn back. Then at last one day, a shout was heard: *"Land ho! Land ho!"*

Ponce ran to the ship's rail. He looked out and saw the long, beautiful coastline ahead. Somehow he felt that this was the place where he would find the Fountain of Youth.

"Get food and guns into the small boats!" he called. The men hurried to do as they were told. They had waited a long time for this moment. Soon they were singing and laughing as they rowed through the waves.

When he set foot on land, Ponce said, "I name this beautiful place 'Florida!'" There were flowers everywhere, and this was a Spanish word meaning "full of flowers."

Ponce and his men set out to look for the magic fountain. Day after day they walked through swamps and woods. Deeper and deeper they went into the wilderness. At times they had to use swords to cut through the thick tangles of vines and branches. And everywhere they went they saw strange birds and animals and beautiful flowers.

The men crossed hundreds of rivers and small streams. At each stream, they would taste the water. Then they would watch each other closely to see if they were growing any younger. But each time they shook their heads sadly and went on.

Ponce and his men marched for a week or more. The hot sun beat down on them. Sharp stones cut through their worn-out boots. Their food supply grew smaller and smaller. The men became more and more unhappy.

Then one morning, someone cried, "Indians up ahead!"

Sure enough, a group of very young Indians were coming toward them through the woods. The Indians had also seen Ponce and his men. They didn't know who these strange people could be, so they quickly hid behind the trees.

One of the sailors tried to speak to the Indians. He used each of the many Indian languages he had learned in the New World. Finally he found one that the Indians seemed to know. With this and some sign language, he asked them about the Fountain of Youth.

One of the Indians smiled and began to speak. He made many signs and drew pictures on the ground.

"The Indian says we must go through the dark forest to find the great fountain," the sailor told Ponce. "He says we must walk until we reach a forest of gold!"

When the sailor said this, his shipmates' eyes opened wide. The sailor went on, "The Indian says that we will see birds of many colors there. If we follow these birds, they will lead us to the fountain."

When he had finished, some of the sailors turned at once and ran straight into the forest. Ponce quickly thanked the young Indian and ran after his crew.

"Do you want to get lost?" he shouted. "We must stay together!" But the men kept running. Ponce shouted again, "Now we'll never know if the Indians were children or old people made young again by the fountain!"

At this the men stopped, although they said nothing. They just got into line and began to march once more. They were too lost in dreams of youth—and of gold.

The blazing sun still beat down from above. The rocks still hurt the men's feet. The branches still scratched them and tore their clothes. But they didn't care about these things now. All that mattered was to keep going. They had to find the golden forest.

At last, when they were almost too tired to take another step, the men saw a great yellow light through the trees. "Gold! Gold!" they cried as they rushed forward. "We've found the forest of gold!"

Again Ponce had to run to catch up with his men. But when he found them, they were sitting on the ground, tired and very sad. Ponce looked up at the leaves of the trees. True, they were a deep yellow, and they blazed like gold in the bright sunshine. But they were just leaves.

Ponce shook his head. "Did you think you would find real gold growing on trees?" he asked.

At that moment, a flock of birds swooped down out of the sky. They settled on the nearby branches. The birds had beautiful feathers of red, green, orange and blue.

The sailors leaped up. "The birds of many colors! The birds of many colors!" they cried. "They'll lead us to the magic fountain!" They were so happy that they began to dance. Some of them shot their guns into the air.

Frightened by the noise, the birds spread their wings and flew away over the treetops. "Come back! Come back!" the sailors begged. But the birds were already out of sight.

The men were quiet once again. Perhaps if they were very, very still, the birds would return. For a long time they sat without making a sound. They waited and waited. Hours passed. But the birds didn't come back. Finally the men knew they would have to go on alone.

Ponce and his men marched and marched. They pushed ahead that whole night and the next day. Some of them began to fear they were lost forever.

But at dawn on the second day, one of the sailors whispered, "Shh! Be quiet. . . ! Do you hear something?" The others held their breath. They listened as hard as they could. Then they cried, "Yes! Yes! We can hear it! It's the sound of water splashing!"

It was too good to be true. The men dashed forward. Packs dropped from their tired backs. Hats fell from their sun-burned heads. "The fountain!" they shouted over and over. "We've found the magic fountain!"

Moments later, the group reached the water. They could see it leaping and splashing for miles around. But it wasn't the wonderful Fountain of Youth. No, what the men saw was the broad blue ocean. They had walked all the way across Florida to the shores of the mighty Atlantic.

Some of the men cried real tears, for now their dreams of youth would never come true. Others stamped and shouted in anger, for now they would never become rich. Only Ponce was silent. "Maybe there is no Fountain of Youth," he said quietly. "But we have had the courage to make the search. And because of this, we will live on, forever young, in the memories of people everywhere."

Juan Ponce de Leon was right. When he died, the people of Puerto Rico built a monument in honor of the great explorer. And this monument still stands, forever young, in the beautiful city of San Juan.

BETTY ZANE,
THE YOUNGEST GENERAL

Vocabulary Preview

dodge   [*DAHJ*]—move aside quickly to get away from something
We saw the player *dodge* as the ball rushed toward him.

keg   [*KEG*]—small barrel
The *keg* was filled with fresh water.

spare   [*SPAIR*]—give up, to get along without
The lady couldn't *spare* even one dime.

target   [*TAR get*]—something to aim at
The arrow hit the *target*.

How many heroes can you name? No doubt you can probably think of several. Many of them are found in the stories in this book.

But does your list include any people who became heroes or heroines when they were still children? The story you are about to read tells of just such a person. Her name was Betty Zane.

Betty was a young girl who was not afraid to face great danger in order to help her people. During the Revolutionary War, she and the other settlers from a small village were trapped in a fort on land that is now Wheeling, West Virginia. The Indians who surrounded the fort had been paid to do so by the British.

What was this unarmed girl's daring plan to save her friends and family from Indian attack? Read this story, and you'll soon find out.

FORT HENRY had been under Indian attack all night. The men and women of the fort were worn out. For hours they had been putting out the fires caused by flaming arrows.

Now it was dawn, and the fighting had stopped for a while. Everything was still. The children in the fort crept out of their hiding places. They could see the arrows stuck in the walls and smell the smoke from the fires. It hung above their heads like a gray cloud.

"Are they gone, Mother?" asked a little boy. "Are we safe now?"

His mother knew they were not safe, but she only said, "Come. There's no time to speak of that. You must have some breakfast."

The boy shook his head. He and the others knew that the

food supply was dangerously low. "No," he said. "The boys and girls have decided not to eat breakfast. That will save lots of food."

General Zane heard what the children had done, and a lump came to his throat. "Men," he said, "even the children are helping now. I'm sure we'll win this fight! All we have to do is hold off the Indians for a few more hours. Help should reach us by then."

But one of the officers shook his head. "A few hours? We can't even hold on for one more hour. We're in real trouble now."

"We need gunpowder," the major continued. "We're helpless without it, and there's barely a pinch left in the whole fort."

The general knew this was true. He sighed, and his face drew into a frown. He paced back and forth, trying to think of a plan.

Suddenly he stopped pacing. His face lit up. "There's a keg of powder in my cabin!" he exclaimed.

The settlers were excited when they heard. A whole keg of powder might be enough to save the day. But then the major spoke up.

"The powder in your cabin? How can that help us? Your cabin's out there, on the other side of the Indians. That's more than a hundred feet from the fort!"

"Let me sneak out. I'll get the powder," offered one young man.

"No," said the general. "You'd be shot down before you were halfway there."

"Let me go! I'm a swift runner," called another. The noise grew as more men begged to be allowed to try.

"Quiet!" cried the general. "We have only eighteen men

left in the entire fort. There are women and children to think of. Not one man can be spared."

The men stared at the ground. Of course the general was right. "We must try to hold the fort," he went on, "without the powder."

Everyone was silent. They were trying to think of a way to save the fort. But then the silence was broken by a small, soft voice.

"Not one man can be spared, that's true," the voice was saying. "But a girl may be spared. Let me go for the keg."

The general turned. There was Betty, his daughter, behind him. "What?" he cried. "Let you go out among the Indians? They'd shoot you on sight!"

But Betty's mind was made up. "I'm your child," she said. "Doesn't that make me almost a soldier too?"

The general stared. He couldn't believe his ears. Betty had always been so frightened of woods and Indians.

But people who are brave are often afraid. And Betty knew what she had to do.

"You *must* let me go," she said. "I can't fire a gun like a soldier, but I can run as fast as one. Please let me try! It's our only chance!"

General Zane knew that the powder might save a lot of lives. He owed it to the others to let her try. At last, with a heavy heart, he said his daughter could go.

The general kissed Betty and held her tight. Then he walked with her to the gate of the fort. But just as the gate was opening, he changed his mind. "I can't do it!" he said. "I can't let you go!" But it was too late. The girl had slipped out through the small opening.

The people in the fort ran to the walls. They looked out through the cracks in the logs. "Poor child," they thought.

"She can't possibly make it. We should never have let her go."

Of course the settlers thought Betty would start running toward the cabin. But instead she did something very strange, and very clever. She walked slowly along as if she were out for a Sunday stroll. She acted as if there were no war going on at all.

Even the Indians were surprised. They didn't know what to make of her actions. Betty stopped to pick a wild flower. Putting it in her hair, she walked calmly on. Soon she reached the cabin and went inside.

A few minutes passed. Then Betty stepped through the doorway holding something wrapped in a blanket. The girl tried not to seem frightened. She stood still for a moment, a perfect target for Indian arrows. But the braves were too puzzled. They simply waited to see what would happen next. Then Betty started to walk slowly back toward the fort.

"She must have clothes in that bundle," said one Indian.

"No," said another. "She wouldn't risk her life for clothes. She must be carrying food or a child."

The brave girl kept on walking. She looked as if nothing special were on her mind. But she kept her eyes on the fort. She could see that she was now halfway there.

The settlers in the fort watched breathlessly. If only nothing happened to spoil the plan! But something did happen. A bird swooped out of the sky right in front of Betty. She was so startled that she dropped what she was carrying. The keg of gunpowder rolled out of the blanket!

Now the Indians saw that they had been tricked. They let out angry yells. Showers of arrows streamed through the air! The girl leaped forward and scooped up the keg. Then she ran toward the fort as fast as she could.

Arrows zipped by. They struck the ground to the right

and left of her. One arrow struck the keg in her arms. "Get her! Get her!" screamed the Indians.

Betty dodged this way and that. Her heart was pounding. She was panting for breath. The fort seemed miles away. "Will I never get there?" she thought.

Still the arrows whizzed by. One tore the flower out of her hair. Betty was growing dizzy with fright. She could feel her legs getting weaker. Then, just as she was about to faint, she saw the gate of the fort a few feet ahead.

Betty threw herself forward in one last, great effort. She almost fell through the half-open gate. *Thud! Thud! Thud!* The arrows hit the huge doors as they closed behind her.

General Zane rushed to his child and threw his arms around her. Tears streamed down his face. "My daughter!" he said. "You're safe! You're safe!"

"And we're safe too!" cried the settlers. "Betty has saved our lives!"

"Three cheers for General Betty, the bravest soldier of them all!" cried the major.

"Three cheers for General Betty!" rang the cry.

Betty smiled happily, but she was too weak to talk. Going to her room, she lay down and closed her eyes. Soon the brave girl was fast asleep. And as she slept she smiled again. It was as if she still heard the thrilling words that had made her so proud: "Three cheers for General Betty, the bravest soldier of them all!"

DANIEL BOONE AND THE
SPIRIT OF THE FOREST

Vocabulary Preview

creature [*KREE cher*]—a living thing, like a person, an animal, a fish, or a bird
The elephant is a huge *creature*.

echo [*EK o*]—repeat of a sound
"Hello!" he shouted into the cave, and the *echo* came back, "Hello!"

muscle [*MUSS l*]—the tissues in our bodies that help us move
The boy used his arm *muscles* to lift himself up to the chinning bar.

spirit [*SPIR it*]—a ghost or fairy
It is said that a *spirit* can go through walls and fly through the air.

Some people say that on Halloween, witches and other evil spirits come to play tricks on frightened humans. Most people laugh at such stories, for not many believe in witches and ghosts any more.

Daniel Boone didn't believe the Indian legends about good and evil spirits either. The Indians thought these spirits lived in the forests and streams, but Daniel knew this wasn't true. Then one day he found himself in the middle of the forest. And he began to wonder if he hadn't been wrong after all.

This is the story of what happened to Daniel Boone on that day.

DANIEL BOONE KNEW all there was to know about hunting. As a boy, he had hunted with the Indians. He had learned a lot from them. He had learned even more on his own. He could tell the footprints of any animal in the woods. And he could trail any creature to its most secret hiding place.

By the time Daniel was a young man, he was famous. His friends would point to him proudly and say, "There goes Daniel Boone, the best hunter in the land!" Why, he had already killed more than fifty bears, and he was just getting started.

Late one afternoon, Daniel set out to kill his fifty-fifth bear. He carried his rifle loaded, so he could fire at any moment. He was taking no chances in the deep, dark forest.

Daniel searched the ground carefully for bear tracks. But there were none in sight. "I wonder," he thought to himself. "Surely all the bears haven't found new hiding places."

Daniel didn't know it, but there were no more bears in

that part of the forest. He had killed the last one the week before. The rain had washed away all the bear tracks that were left.

Daniel scratched his head. "I just don't understand it," he said. "This is supposed to be bear country." But he wouldn't give up the hunt. He kept searching until shadows filled the woods.

At last Daniel sighed and started for home. He walked until he was near the edge of the forest. Suddenly he stopped in his tracks! What was that sound? Daniel stood very still, listening. Sure enough, he heard it again!

Crick-crack! Someone or something had stepped on a dry twig. The sound seemed to come from a grove of small trees straight ahead. Were Indians hiding there? Or was a wild beast ready to leap out at him?

Daniel didn't move a muscle. He was as still as one of the trees. He waited.

Ten minutes passed. The shadows were growing deeper and deeper. Another ten minutes went by. "Maybe it was just a falling branch," thought Daniel. "Or maybe I was just hearing things."

Then, *crick-crack!* The strange sound echoed again! This time Daniel threw himself to the ground. He aimed his gun at the trees. Then his heart leaped to his throat, for he saw *two big green eyes* staring out at him!

Bright as green fire, the eyes shone through the darkness. Daniel knew that neither bears nor Indians had eyes like that. He wondered if perhaps the Indian legends might be true. Perhaps ghosts and spirits *did* live in the woods.

"Maybe that's why there were no bears," he thought. "Maybe a terrible spirit has chased them away. And maybe that spirit is now after *me!*"

The young hunter knew he couldn't escape. He'd have to face whatever was hiding among the trees. His finger on the trigger, he crawled closer.

It was now or never! Daniel jumped to his feet and ran toward the trees. He went straight up to the branches. Through the leaves, the green eyes still stared at him. Daniel aimed his gun right between the glowing eyes.

Then, just as he was about to pull the trigger, a small voice cried, "No! No! Don't shoot me, please!"

Daniel froze in his tracks. "What's this?" he thought. "What kind of spirit speaks English? And says *please?*"

The branches parted, and out stepped one of the loveliest creatures Daniel had ever seen. Slowly he lowered his gun. He thought of the Indian tales about beautiful and good spirits who lived in the streams. Was this one of those spirits?

The creature stepped closer to Daniel. His jaw dropped. It was a beautiful girl, no more than sixteen. And she had the most beautiful bright green eyes he had ever seen. They sparkled and shone like jewels.

"Why—why didn't you speak up sooner?" Daniel asked. "I might have killed you!"

The girl's voice trembled. "I thought you might be a bear or an Indian," she said. "I was so frightened. I didn't dare come out until you were close enough for me to see you."

Daniel smiled and shook his head. He hoped she would go on talking. Her voice was so sweet and soft. But the girl just looked at him shyly, so Daniel spoke up.

"Well, what brought you into the woods in the first place?" he asked.

"Today is my father's birthday," she said. "I was looking for wild berries so I could make him a pie. I guess I didn't watch where I was going. Before I knew it, I was lost."

"Your family must be new in these parts," Daniel said. "I know I've never seen *you* before."

The girl blushed. "We've just settled here," she said. "Our cabin is only half built."

"So those are your folks down by the stream! I was planning to get over there this week to welcome you and give you a hand."

The two young people began to walk through the woods. "Better give me your hand," said Daniel. "You might trip over a rock in these shadows." He was glad it was too dark for her to see his red face.

Soon they reached the trail outside the woods. The night was still, except for the sound of their footsteps. They walked along, hand in hand.

The half-built cabin soon appeared in the distance. Looking at it, Daniel quickly promised himself two things. First he promised he'd help the new family to finish their home. Then he promised he'd build himself a brand-new home right near that big oak tree he liked so much. He looked down into the green eyes and smiled. They were smiling back.

Oh, Daniel hadn't caught a bear that day. But he had caught himself something much more exciting and important. You see, he had captured the heart of a beautiful green-eyed creature who was soon to be his wife.

DANIEL BOONE,
FIRST DETECTIVE OF THE
OLD FRONTIER

Vocabulary Preview

chores   [*CHORZ*]—jobs to be done
Feeding the chickens was one of the boy's *chores.*

clue   [*KLOO*]—any small thing that helps find the answer to a problem
The police searched for a *clue* to help them find the thief.

mischief   [*MISS chif*]—playful misbehavior
Although Jim behaved in public, he often got into *mischief* at home.

paddle   [*PAD l*]—a stick of wood that is flattened at one end; a short oar
He used a *paddle* to get the canoe across the lake.

prisoner   [*PRIZ i ner*]—a person held against his will
The man was held *prisoner* by the pirates.

shriek   [*SHREEK*]—a loud, high scream
The girl began to *shriek* when she saw the fire.

You would probably have trouble picking out a detective on the street. Just for fun, try to tell in one sentence why this might be so.

When people see pictures of Daniel Boone, they usually think of him as a scout, a hunter, a pioneer or a trapper. But have you ever heard that Daniel Boone was a detective? Probably not.

And yet Daniel was a very fine detective. He was a master at spotting clues, tracking down animals, finding missing people and uncovering Indian secrets.

The story you are about to read explains how Daniel solved the case of the missing children.

DANIEL BOONE HAD LONG HEARD TALES about the wilds of Kentucky. One day he made up his mind to see the strange land for himself. He put some food and clothing into a leather bag, picked up his gun and set out.

After a few days' travel, Daniel was climbing the green hills of Kentucky. He crossed clear streams and wide rivers. He cut his way through thick forests. "This is a rich new world," he thought. "I'll bring my family and friends to this beautiful country. It will be our new home."

Daniel did just that. Soon a whole group of settlers had built their homes near a river in the new land. They named their town Boonesboro. They were happy there, and their settlement grew and grew.

But the Indians weren't happy. They felt that the land belonged to them. They tried to make the settlers leave. Time and time again, the Indians attacked the settlement. But each time they were pushed back. This only made them angrier.

When the Indians weren't around, though, Boonesboro was a pleasant place. The men hunted and fished and took care of the crops. The women cooked, made soap and sewed clothes for their families. The children did their chores, studied their lessons and had the rest of the time for play.

One evening, after their work was done, two of the young girls of the village went for a walk. One of them was Daniel's teen-age daughter. She was a beautiful, dark-eyed girl who was full of mischief. "I know," she said to her friend. "Let's go out beyond the town. We can catch frogs near the river."

"But we're not supposed to leave the village," said her friend. "It would be fun, though. All right, let's go!"

So the girls sneaked down to the river. They saw Daniel's canoe on the bank. "I dare you to go for a ride!" said Daniel's daughter.

Soon the girls were paddling the boat out into the river. They couldn't handle the big paddles very well, however, and the boat began to drift. The girls were too frightened to call for help. Besides, they knew they'd be punished if their parents found out what they had done.

Just then the girls felt something bump against the side of the canoe. They looked down into the water. Were they seeing things? *No!* There was an Indian swimming right beside them! He grabbed one side of the canoe and steered it toward the shore.

When the boat touched the riverbank, three more Indians appeared. They had been hiding in the branches of a tree. They made a sign to the girls warning them not to scream.

The Indians had been waiting for a chance like this. Now they would hold the girls captive until the settlers agreed to leave their land. The braves were even happier that one of their prisoners was the daughter of the great Daniel Boone.

One of the Indians cut a small branch and brushed it over the tracks around the tree. Then he and his friends led the frightened girls through the woods. The braves moved swiftly. They knew that Daniel Boone would soon be after them.

Back at Boonesboro, a boy ran to Daniel's house. He had seen the girls leave the village and had followed them. "Your daughter and her friend have gone off in your canoe," he cried.

Daniel ran down to the riverbank and saw that his boat was gone. Worried, he searched for clues to help solve the problem.

First he looked to see which way the water was moving. Then he ran along the bank in that direction. Soon he caught sight of the empty canoe, stuck among the rocks.

"Oh, no!" he thought. "Maybe the girls have fallen into the river!" He was just about to dive into the water when he noticed a few green leaves on the ground under a tree. Now, Daniel knew that leaves don't fall by themselves in mid-summer. He looked up at the tree. He saw that the leaves and branches had been disturbed. He also saw that one small branch had been cut off.

There was no time to lose! Daniel knew now that he was dealing with Indians. He stepped quickly into the shadows of the woods.

Daniel had a plan. He knew the country better than the Indians thought he knew it. He found an old Indian trail that he was sure the braves were using. Without making a sound, he crept through the trees growing along the narrow path.

The great scout was careful not to move too swiftly. He

didn't want the Indians to know that he was after them. He feared that if they saw or heard him they might kill the girls and run off.

An hour passed. "The Indians must think they're safe by this time," thought Daniel. "They've stopped brushing over their tracks. It's time for me to try to get closer."

Daniel began to move faster. He listened carefully to every sound. He kept his eyes on the tracks the careless Indians were now leaving. He felt lucky to have found the right trail. But then, to his great surprise, the tracks went off the narrow path and into the forest!

What was going on? Had the Indians heard him and decided to take another trail? Were they hiding in the trees, waiting to leap down on him? And what about the girls? Were they still safe?

Daniel quickly looked up. But there were no Indians in the trees around him. He began following the tracks into the forest. He knew that he might be walking into a trap.

The great hunter didn't know it, but the Indians weren't too far away. They hadn't seen or heard anyone chasing them, so they had decided it was safe to stop for a rest.

The girls were glad for a chance to sit down. They were out of breath, and their feet hurt. The unhappy girls took off their shoes and sat under a tree. They watched a brave gather some twigs and start a fire. Soon a small blaze was glowing brightly, and all the braves sat around it. They were laughing and talking about their day's adventure.

"Our chief will be pleased that we have captured the child of the mighty Daniel Boone," said one of the braves.

"Yes," laughed another. "Perhaps the great hunter is calling right now for his daughter to come home for the evening meal." The other braves laughed at this.

The sound of their laughter echoed through the woods and reached Daniel's ears. He followed the sound to a thick grove of trees. From there he could see the glow from the small fire burning just beyond. He looked through the leafy branches and saw the girls sitting under a tree. Then he saw the Indians seated around the fire. It was time for his plan.

Daniel smeared his face with earth so that only his bright eyes and pale hair shone through. With the help of the firelight, he looked terrible indeed. Then he began to wail and moan as fearfully as he could.

"*Aiee! Help!*" one of the Indians shrieked. "*A forest spirit! A forest spirit!*" The other braves jumped to their feet and looked toward the trees. Daniel knew that there wasn't a second to waste. With a fierce yell, he leaped into the open. His rifle blazing, he rushed toward the Indians. One of the braves tumbled to the ground.

"The great hunter! The great hunter!" cried the other braves. Their screams of terror filled the air.

"There was no one behind us on the trail!" cried one Indian. "He must have flown over the tops of the trees like a bird!"

"Surely a forest spirit carried the great hunter right to our fire!" howled another Indian as he and the other braves ran off. They had forgotten all about their two prisoners. They were afraid Daniel would be racing after them.

But Daniel Boone didn't bother to chase the Indians. He hurried over to the shaking girls and helped them to their feet.

"Father! Father!" cried Daniel's daughter. "How did you find us? Where did you come from?"

"There's no time for questions now," said Daniel. "Quick! Put on your shoes! Let's get out of here!"

He led the two back through the forest. The sound of a

trickling stream helped to guide them through the dark woods toward the river. Hours later, they reached the other side of the forest.

Soon the girls were safe at home. With tears in their eyes, they said over and over how sorry they were for the trouble they had caused.

After that adventure, the girls never left Boonesboro without permission. You can bet on that! And the Indians didn't attack the settlement for a long, long time. They were sure that the forest spirits were friends of the mighty Daniel Boone.

MIKE FINK
AND THE RIVER PIRATES

Vocabulary Preview

coward   [*KOW erd*]—person afraid to face danger
The *coward* ran to hide when the battle started.

keelboat   [*KEEL boat*]—boat that is heavy on the bottom so that it won't tip over
The *keelboat* carried cargo up and down the river.

shriek   [*SHREEK*]—sharp scream
John let out a *shriek* when he stubbed his toe.

situation   [*sit u A shun*]—the way things are
He didn't like the *situation*, but there was nothing he could do to change it.

stowaway   [*STO a way*]—person who hides on a boat to travel without paying
The *stowaway* was found hiding in a cabin on the boat.

Usually we think that a story has either a happy ending or a sad one. In the next story, however, you will read about a person who felt both happy *and* sad at the way an event turned out.

How can a person feel both happy and sad? To answer that question, all you have to do is think of how mothers cry at their daughters' weddings!

Here is another example. You would be sad to say good-by to your best friend if he or she were going on a very long vacation. At the same time, you'd be glad to know your friend was going to have a wonderful time.

See if you can think of any other "glad-sad" situations.

Now, as you read, you will be able to understand why Mike Fink, greatest of the keelboat captains, felt both glad and sad about the outcome of one of his strangest adventures.

"WHAT? THERE'S A STOWAWAY ON BOARD?" roared Mike Fink. He shook his huge fists. "There'll be no stowaways on my keelboat! Bring him here! I'll throw him over the side!"

But Mike had a surprise coming. "A *girl* stowaway?" he shouted. "That's not possible!"

It was true, though. There *was* a girl on Mike's boat. She was about seventeen years old, and *very* pretty. And her name was Aurelia.

Aurelia fixed her big blue eyes on Mike. "I know that you don't allow women on your trips up the Ohio," she said. "But I must get to Pittsburgh. That's why I sneaked on board and hid."

"But this is the Ohio River!" Mike snapped. "Don't you know there are pirates on this river? It's no place for a girl!"

The girl smiled sweetly and took out her small fan. "Oh, Captain Fink," she said, "you know the pirates don't attack the *Lightfoot*. They run and hide as soon as they see the red feather in your hat."

Mike grinned foolishly. No one had ever called him *Captain* Fink before. "Won't you take me with you to Pittsburgh?" the girl went on. "I have business to take care of there for my family. It's *very* important."

Now Mike liked the girl's courage, as well as her blue eyes. He also liked being called Captain Fink. So he thought a bit, and then he said, "Oh, all right. You can come along this time. But stay out of the way—and don't go falling overboard!"

The boat moved along up the river. The crew worked busily, and Mike hummed a jolly tune. Little did any of them guess that they'd soon be face to face with trouble.

Meanwhile, a few miles up the river, in the pirates' cave at Cave-in-Rock, two men were fighting.

"That ring is mine," cried Tall Ned. "I took it from the dead man's hand. Give it back to me, I say!"

"No!" shouted the other pirate. "The ring is mine. I'm the one who killed the man."

"We'll see about that," said Tall Ned. He pulled out his knife and knocked over the table. "Get ready to die," he sneered.

Suddenly their captain entered the cave. His eyes blazed like fire. "All right, Tall Ned," he growled. "I told you what would happen if I caught you fighting over treasure again. Now you'll hang!"

Captain Camilla ordered two strong men to drag Ned out. He told them to hang him from a tall tree on the cliff overlooking the river. "And hang him high," he snarled. "Make him dance in the air!"

"One more chance," begged Ned. "Give me one more chance!"

"No!" snapped the captain. "Last week you shot one of our best men in a fight over some gold. Next week it'll be someone else. No more chances, I say!"

The two pirates dragged Ned out to the edge of the cliff. Tall Ned knew he must think of a plan or lose his life. So, while the two men were fixing the rope, he fell shrieking to the ground. He hid his face and cried like a baby. He moaned and groaned for all he was worth. The pirates laughed to hear him sobbing. But while they were laughing, Ned suddenly leaped over the cliff. He hit the water with a splash.

Now the two pirates were scared. Captain Camilla was very cruel. They knew he'd have *them* hanged if he learned that Ned had escaped. So they went back to the cave and told the captain that Ned had been killed and thrown into the river.

Just then, a lookout ran into the cave. "There's a keelboat coming up the river," he cried. It was the *Lightfoot*. The captain smiled wickedly, and his eyes gleamed. He ordered his men to get ready to sail.

Ten minutes later, the pirate boat was heading down the river. Captain Camilla stood like a king on the deck. The Jolly Roger fluttered in the breeze.

Soon the two boats were in sight of each other. Shouting through a horn, the pirate captain warned, "Ahoy! Give up! Don't put up a fight or you're all dead men!"

The boats drew closer and closer to each other. Tall and proud, Mike Fink raised his gun. "This is my answer to you," he yelled. He took careful aim. First one bullet, then a second, whistled through the air. They headed straight for the Jolly Roger. The bullets ripped through the eye-holes of the skull-and-crossbones as neatly as you please!

The pirates were speechless! Captain Camilla cried, "There's just one man who can shoot like that——"

Mike Fink roared with laughter and stuck the red feather back into his hat. (He'd been hiding it all the time.)

"Ya-hoo, you river rats!" he yelled. "I'm a land-screamer! I'm a water dog! I'm a snapping turtle! I can lick my weight in wildcats! I can out-run, out-dance, out-shoot and out-fight any man alive! *Now* do you know who I am?"

"It's Mike Fink!" screamed the pirates. Mike howled with laughter as more than a dozen of them leaped into the water like frogs.

"Come back, you cowards," cried Captain Camilla. But not one of the men swam back to the boat. Then the Captain saw Tall Ned. He was standing next to Mike, laughing.

"So," shouted the captain, "you're not dead after all, you snake-in-the-grass! It was *you* who warned Mike Fink that we were near." He raised his gun and aimed it at Tall Ned.

Mike swiftly took aim. POW! He shot the pirate's bullet right out of the air! Mike went on shooting, for the boats were now touching, and the pirates were leaping to the deck of the *Lightfoot*.

Shouts, groans and the sound of clashing knives filled the air. Wounded men fell overboard on every side. Others fell bleeding to the deck. Mike was all over the ship during the bloody fight. If it hadn't been for his great skill with a gun, things would have gone badly for the crew of the *Lightfoot*.

But soon the pirates were beaten. All were either dead or swimming away to safety. Mike was so pleased with himself that he danced a jig. However, he stopped dancing and ran to the rail when he saw what was happening on shore.

What Mike saw was Captain Camilla, running toward the woods beyond the river. And he was dragging Aurelia along behind him! The cruel captain had pulled the girl over the side with him when he jumped from Mike's boat.

Camilla was now safe in the woods. But though he was out of sight, his voice could be heard shouting to Mike. "Gold," called Camilla. "Leave gold on the shore tomorrow morning if you want to get the girl back. If you don't. . . ."

Mike heard no more.

The keelboat captain was fit to be tied. He paced back and forth, muttering to himself. "We've got to rescue Aurelia," he said. "But how? How?" Then his eyes fell on Tall Ned.

"You!" he snapped. "You know where Camilla's hideout is. Tonight, when it's dark, you're going to lead us there."

The thought of seeing Captain Camilla again didn't make Tall Ned exactly happy. But nothing he could say would change Mike Fink's mind. Finally Tall Ned sighed and gave in. He even thought of a plan.

"Camilla is probably watching us from behind those trees," the pirate said. "Let's take the boat farther up the river so he'll think we're leaving. I know a place where we can hide the boat safely and then sneak up on him."

"You'd better be right," growled Mike. "Let's get started. It's almost dark now."

Ned was true to his word. He showed Mike a secret place to hide the *Lightfoot*. Then he led the men through the dark woods and up the rocky hillside. The first sounds that reached their ears were the loud voices of the pirates shouting and singing in their cave. Mike and his men could see the glow of firelight inside the hideout.

Then Ned pointed to a wooden hut farther up the hill. "That's Captain Camilla's own place," he said. "He has never let any of his men set foot inside it."

But Mike wasn't listening. He and his men were creeping

toward the cave. Just as they reached the entrance, out walked Captain Camilla! Mike fired a bullet straight at the captain. Camilla jumped back, but he didn't fall. The bullet had hit the knife he was wearing in his belt.

"Out with the lights, and follow me!" Camilla shouted to his men as he ran back into the cave. He quickly led the pirates out through another opening.

"After them!" cried Mike. Whooping and yelling, Mike's men followed. They ran through the cave and out the other side, firing their guns as they ran. Pirate after pirate fell—all except Camilla. No one saw where he had gone. He had run back to his hut.

"Look up there," shouted Ned to Mike suddenly. "Do you see what I see?"

"Fire!" cried Mike. "Camilla's hut is on fire! Come on! Aurelia may be in there!" The men sped toward the burning hut.

"Ha, ha, ha!" laughed a voice ahead of them. Mike saw Camilla standing on the roof of the burning building. "Fools!" Camilla cried. "This is my answer to you! The girl is in the hut. Now she and I will die together!" He leaped from the roof and ran back into the burning hut.

Mike climbed quickly up the hillside. By the time he pushed open the door of the hut, great waves of fire leaped out at him.

"Too late," Mike groaned. "We're too late!"

Mike had never cried before, but now tears filled his eyes. He stood staring at the flames. Then he heard a voice he knew calling for help. It was Aurelia's voice, and it was coming from the woods below.

In the light of the flames, Mike saw Camilla dragging Aurelia down the hill toward the shore. And Mike saw something else—something very strange. A tiny figure all in white seemed to be floating behind Camilla. Was it a ghost?

Mike and his men hurried down the hill after Camilla. They wondered how he had escaped from the hut.

"He probably jumped out the back window and pulled the girl after him," said Tall Ned.

Mike agreed. "But we have no time to talk now," he said. "Look, Camilla has almost reached the shore. And there's a boat in the water."

Camilla stopped at the shore for a few seconds and looked back. As he did, the little figure in white flew past him and climbed into the boat. Then the tiny creature hid under a blanket in the front of the boat.

Camilla saw Mike and his crew hurrying down the hillside. He dragged the screaming Aurelia into the boat and began rowing as fast as he could.

"You'll never catch me," he screamed like a madman.

Mike was out of breath when he reached the shore. He raised his rifle to shoot at Captain Camilla.

"Be careful you don't hit the girl," warned one of his men.

Mike took careful aim and fired the gun. The bullet whistled over the water. "Agh!" cried Camilla. "You've hit me! But I'll get even with you, Mike Fink!" Camilla rocked the boat until it turned over in the deep water.

"The girl will drown," cried Mike. He jumped into the river and swam toward the overturned boat with all his might. He reached Aurelia just in time to save her.

As he swam with her toward the shore, he looked back. The little figure in white was now holding Camilla around the neck. Was it a ghost trying to drag him under to punish him for his evil deeds?

"Help! Help!" cried Camilla. "I'm too weak to swim. Come back and save my little girl!"

"So *that's* why Camilla never let us inside his hut," exclaimed Tall Ned. "He had his little daughter living there with him!"

Mike handed Aurelia to the men on shore. Then he started back to save Camilla's child. She was still dressed in her white nightgown. Mike could hear Camilla crying, "Oh, my daughter, you should have stayed where I told you. I would have come back for you. I didn't know you were following me!"

Mike had almost reached them, when a terrible thing happened. Camilla screamed once, and sank beneath the water. It was the last time Captain Camilla and his child were ever seen.

"What a terrible price Camilla has paid for his crimes," whispered Mike to himself. "A terrible price!" He swam slowly back to shore.

When the sun rose the next morning, the *Lightfoot* was already sailing up the broad Ohio. The keelboat moved along as smoothly and quietly as if nothing had happened to delay its journey. Standing up front, next to a beautiful blue-eyed girl, was its mighty captain, Mike Fink. And in his hat, dancing in the breeze, was a bright red feather.

SECRET AGENT M

code   [*KODE*]—words or signals used for sending secret messages

The man didn't understand the letter because he didn't know the *code* that was being used.

conductor   [*kon DUK ter*]—one who looks after people on a bus or train

The *conductor* asked to see the man's ticket.

former   [*FOR mer*]—past

The teacher was visited by her *former* pupils.

heroic   [*hee RO ik*]—brave

The child's *heroic* deed was being talked about by everyone.

heroine   [*HAIR o in*]—a brave lady or girl

Harriet Tubman was a great *heroine*.

military   [*MIL i tair ee*]—having to do with the armed services

A general is a *military* man.

wisdom   [*WIZ dum*]—very good judgment

People asked the old man for advice because he was known for his *wisdom*.

Can you figure out the message in the following sentence? Don't read beyond it until you have tried to break its code all by yourself.

Robert, Ed and Dan need old wire.

Have you figured it out? If you have, you guessed that you should put together the first letters of the words to form the two-word message: *READ NOW.*

Many legends have grown up around Harriet Tubman's use of code letters and clever tricks to get her important work done. The tale that follows is based on some of the stories told about this great lady's daring adventures. Read to find out how she took risk after risk, and used trick after trick, to perform her heroic tasks.

"FORTY THOUSAND DOLLARS for one runaway slave?" asked a man. "That's a mighty big reward for one little lady!"

His friend laughed. "That little lady you're talking about has led more than sixty runaway slaves up North," he said. "And she's still at it!"

The first man nodded. "Now I understand," he said. Then he looked at the poster again. "It says that she can't read or write," he added.

The men didn't notice the lady who had stopped to listen to them, and to look at the poster. Her own picture was on it! "That poster is about *me*," she whispered to herself. When the men started to turn around, she quickly stooped to the ground and picked up a newspaper. She held it as though she were reading it. "I hope the paper is right side up," she thought, as the men looked at her.

"No," said one of the men. "That can't be Harriet Tubman. Can't you see she's reading?"

The paper shook in Harriet's hands as she walked away. "That was close," she sighed. Then she turned the corner and walked quickly toward a large gray house. It was the home of a white friend.

Harriet went into the kitchen, nodding to her friend. Then she climbed a ladder to a small door in the ceiling. She knocked three times. "It's *M*," she whispered.

The door opened, and six former slaves climbed down the ladder. "It's beginning to get dark. Tonight we'll cross into a free state," Harriet said. "Now get your things. Your trip on the Underground Railroad is almost over."

Of course, Harriet Tubman was not taking these people on a real railroad. The Underground Railroad was the code name for the path that slaves took on their trip to freedom. Each hideout along the way was called a station. And the person who did the leading was called the conductor. Harriet was one of the most famous conductors.

Soon Harriet and her six passengers were ready to leave. Before they left the house, Harriet went outside to be sure no one was around. To her horror, she saw the sheriff and some of his men come riding up the road just as she stepped onto the porch.

"Hey, you!" the sheriff shouted. "You're new around here! What's your name?"

Harriet's white friend came out to the porch carrying a broom. "Here!" she shouted at Harriet. "Start sweeping! And don't take half the night doing it!" Harriet took the broom and began to sweep the front steps. Of course, she kept her head down all the while.

"And stop bothering my servant," called Harriet's friend

to the sheriff. "Can't you see she's got work to do?"

The sheriff tipped his hat to the lady. "Just doing my job ma'am," he called. "Sorry to have troubled you." Then he and his men rode off.

Later that night, Harriet threw a shawl over her head and led her "passengers" out through the dark streets. Soon the group was outside the city and in the country. Running through the woods, Harriet led the people to a stream. "Freedom is on the other side of this water," she said. "Come on."

Half an hour later the former slaves were on the free soil of Pennsylvania. One of them, a girl only thirteen years old, was so happy that she began to cry.

Then a stranger stepped out from behind a tree. "Is that you, *M*?" he called softly.

"Yes, it is," whispered Harriet. "You're right on time. Take these people to the next station. I've got to start back to Maryland right away."

"Won't you change your mind and come with us?" a woman asked Harriet.

Harriet shook her head. "I'm told that my people were from Ashanti country in Africa," she laughed. "And you must have heard that the Ashantis don't change their minds easily once they're made up."

Harriet saw that her friends looked sad. "Anyway," she went on, "this time I'm going back to get my brothers." Then the people knew that nothing they could say would make her change her mind.

Soon she was on her way back to Maryland. As she traveled, she wondered what tricks she could use this time to help her brothers escape. She thought and thought. Finally she knew what she would do.

That night, Harriet asked a friend to write a letter for her. The letter was sent to Jacob Jackson, a white man who knew her brothers well. She knew that he would understand the strange message.

The letter had Jacob's name on it. But that didn't keep the postmaster from opening it. He thought Jacob might be one of the people who helped slaves to run away, so he read all of Jacob's mail first. Puzzled, the postmaster scratched his head as he read the message:

Tell my brothers to be always watching, and when the ship comes along, be ready to step on board.
William Henry Jackson

The postmaster knew that William Henry Jackson was Jacob's son who lived up North, but William had no brothers or sisters. What brothers could he be writing about? Finally the postmaster sent for Jacob to explain the letter.

Jacob looked at it for a long time. "You're right," he said. "This is a strange message. I'm sure it wasn't meant for me."

Of course the postmaster thought Jacob was lying. But in truth, Jacob knew the message *wasn't* for him!

Jacob knew the message was for Harriet's brothers. He had to take it to them right away. He knew how glad they'd be to hear about the escape plan. The parents of the two men would be happy too. Jacob wished he could tell them the news. But the two old people lived in a cabin many miles away.

Harriet's brothers had been taken from their parents years before. Now the men were slaves on farms not far from Jacob's home. So Jacob was able to see each of them that very night.

"I've got important news for you," he told Ben, Henry and

John Tubman. "Your sister will be here to take you away soon. Moses is going to lead you to freedom!"

"Moses?" asked Ben. "Did you say Moses?"

Jacob nodded. "That's your sister's code name," he explained. "Now, don't forget to keep your eyes and ears open for the signal to start North."

The brothers didn't forget. And soon they received another message. Ben and Henry did just what it said to do. On Saturday, the day before Christmas, they sneaked over to the old cabin in which they were to meet their sister. She was there with the others who were escaping on the Underground Railroad.

The two brothers hugged Harriet, and tears filled their eyes. "It's so good to see you," cried Harriet. "But where's brother John?"

"I guess John's going to be late," answered Henry.

Harriet shook her head sadly. "We can't wait for him. The danger is too great. We must leave now."

With a heavy heart, Harriet led her passengers out of the old cabin. She led them many miles through the woods and along secret roads. As night fell, the group reached a fodder house, a small cabin in which corn for animals was stored. Soon Harriet and her passengers were safe inside.

In no time at all, everyone but Harriet was asleep on the piles of corn. She was still awake just before dawn when John, her third brother, rapped lightly on the door. Harriet didn't know how he had found them. The important thing was that he had. Now the brothers and sister were all together at last.

Later that morning, the sleepy-eyed group saw Harriet standing at the window. She was looking at a nearby cabin. It was her parents' home!

Poor Harriet! How she longed to rush into the cabin and

throw her arms around her parents. But she couldn't risk it. She was afraid that her mother would cry out and perhaps call attention to what was happening. But she had to let her mother and father know that she was safe, and that her brothers would soon be free. So she asked one of the men in the group to speak to her father.

The man tiptoed up to the cabin. He called the white-haired man outside. "Your children are hiding in the fodder house," he said. "But don't let your wife know. We can't take the chance of being found out."

The old man listened in silence. Then he did a strange thing. First he got some supplies from the cabin. Then he went to the fodder house and pushed them through the door. When he had done this, he left. Harriet and her brothers smiled. They knew why their father wouldn't come inside.

Later that rainy Christmas night, the old man returned to push more food through the door. This time he heard Harriet's soft voice calling, "We're coming out. It's time to leave."

With shaking hands, the old man quickly tied a handkerchief over his eyes. Blindfolded, he hugged each of his children in turn. He didn't see their faces. Then he went quickly through the rain to his own cabin.

Late that night a band of men rode up to the door of the old man's cabin. They didn't even get off their horses. Kicking open the door, one man cried, "Your sons have run off, old man. Have you seen them?"

Harriet's father shook his head. "No," he said. "I haven't seen my boys in more than a week. And that's the truth!" Knowing that the old man was honest, the men rode off.

Harriet's father was out of danger, but the danger was just beginning for Harriet, her brothers and the people who were with them. The group pushed on all that wet night through a huge swamp. Great mudholes and snakes were everywhere. But Harriet showed no fear. Finally it stopped raining, and the sky cleared. "Keep your eyes on the North Star," Harriet told everyone. "We're going to follow the North Star to freedom!"

At dawn, Harriet and her passengers had reached the woods on the other side of the swamp. Harriet sang hymns to cheer her weary followers. But one man wouldn't be cheered up. "I'm just too tired," he moaned. "You can sing all you want to, but I have to rest." Then he sat down under a tree and refused to move.

Still singing, Harriet walked over to the big man. She rolled up her sleeves. The others stared. What was their little leader going to do?

Without missing a note of her hymn, Harriet reached down and took hold of the man by his big shoulders. With one yank, she pulled him to his feet. Her years as a farm worker had made her very strong. The huge man just stood there, his mouth open.

After that, no one complained of being tired. They followed Harriet up and down steep hills. They crossed streams and crawled under fences. On and on they hurried, from one station to the next.

At last, weak and hungry, they set foot in a free state. One passenger stayed on. Harriet took two others to friends in New York. Then she led her brothers all the way to Canada.

But Harriet didn't stay in Canada with them. She had more work to do. She went down South again and again. No one knows for sure just how many hundreds of men, women and children Harriet Tubman led to freedom.

Years later, Harriet served as a Union nurse in the Civil War. After the war, when all the slaves were free, she settled down in Auburn, New York. As the years passed, many people came to see the aging heroine.

One day in 1913, the mayor of Auburn heard sad news. Harriet Tubman, the Moses of her people, had died. The mayor asked all the citizens of the town to hang out flags in her honor. Soon the Stars and Stripes could be seen flying from every home in Auburn. This military honor was only fitting. For in her lifetime, Harriet Tubman had shown the wisdom of a general and the courage of a whole army of fighting men.

JOHN HENRY
AND THE MONSTER

Vocabulary Preview

cradle   [*KRAY dl*]—a baby's bed with rockers
The mother rocked the *cradle* until the baby fell asleep.

determined   [*di TER mend*]—to have your mind strongly made up about something
The boy was *determined* to win the race.

drill   [*DRIL*]—to make holes with a tool or a machine
The men started to *drill* through the rock.

Americans aren't quitters! Thomas Edison wouldn't stop until he had made his electric light work. Admiral Peary wouldn't turn back until he had reached the North Pole. Can you think of other Americans who wouldn't give up until they had reached their goals?

John Henry was one. He was a man well known for his great strength. He was also known for his desire to help make our land great. John Henry did more than his share to put America on wheels of steel. And he wouldn't give up until he had done all he could.

This is his story. After you read it, you will remember it, and John Henry's name, for a long time to come.

THE WORKERS couldn't believe their eyes! They watched as the little boy swung the great hammer around and around in the air. Then, CRASH! Little John Henry drove the spike through the wooden railroad tie with one stroke of the hammer! Not even a grown man had ever been able to do that.

The men were amazed. "That's something, little John!" they exclaimed. "You'll be a famous man when you grow up!"

The workers were right. When the Civil War was over, the nation needed more and more railroads. John Henry became famous for the miles of track he could lay down in a single day. What a worker he was! With a hammer in each hand, he would run between a set of rails and drive in spike after spike on either side.

In the evening, John loved to walk along the railroad tracks. His wife Polly would walk with him. They'd listen to the train whistles and watch the trains go rushing past.

One night John made up his mind to take a long train ride. "Polly," he said, "let's go to West Virginia. They're drilling the Big Bend Tunnel out there. I'd like to help."

"I'll go anywhere that'll make you happy," said Polly. So they went home and began to make their plans. Before many days had passed, they were on their way.

John and Polly were happy in their new home in West Virginia. John liked his new job, and the workers liked John. Everything was just fine.

Then one day a man from the city came to the camp. He showed the boys a machine. "This is a steam drill," said the salesman. "It can drill holes into rock faster than any man."

The boss just laughed. "You don't know John Henry," he said. "He can do as much work as ten men, in half the time!"

The man from the city didn't like that kind of talk. It was bad for business. So he said, "I'll bet my machine can beat your John Henry. In fact, if John Henry beats my machine in a race, you can keep the machine *for free!*"

John had heard everything the two men had said. Now he walked over to his boss. "Go ahead and take the bet," he laughed. "We'll win the machine and give it to my son for a toy."

The boss took the bet at once. "Be here in the morning," he told the salesman. "And bring your monster with you!"

News of the contest spread far and wide. People started to pour into camp early the next day. They all wanted to see John Henry beat the monster.

And the machine did look like a monster! It was big and noisy and ugly. It rumbled and shook, and it sent great puffs of steam into the air. Everyone gathered around to look at it.

Then, suddenly, there was a loud roar. "Here comes John Henry!" the people shouted. "Make way! Make way!" Sure enough, there were John and Polly, and in Polly's arms was their baby son.

People stepped aside to clear a path for the three. As they walked toward the crowd, Polly put her hand on John Henry's great arm. She was worried. "Dear husband," she whispered. "You've been working so hard lately. Perhaps you should rest before you try to beat such a powerful machine. Tell the man to come back next week."

John Henry only laughed. He laughed so hard that he woke up the baby. John reached out and took his tiny son in one hand. The baby looked even smaller in his father's huge palm.

The crowd was still. Only the hissing of the steam drill broke the silence. John moved his hand gently back and forth, like a rocking cradle. Soon the baby was asleep again. John handed the child back to Polly.

"Rest is for babies," John whispered softly. His wife said no more. She gave the baby to a friend to take back to the house. Then Polly smiled at her husband and took his arm. They walked up to the waiting crowd.

Now the contest was about to begin. John Henry was to drive a long drill into the side of the mountain. A few yards away, the man from the city was to do the same with his rumbling, puffing machine.

Bang! A shot rang out. The contest was on! Both men tore right in. The muscles on John Henry's arms stood out like huge loaves of bread. He swung his hammers, one in each hand. *Clang, clang, clang!* The hammers beat the steel drill into the rock inch by inch.

The machine wasn't still for a moment either. It pounded furiously through the rock.

Whoosh-bang! Whoosh-bang! went John's hammers.

Ker-chug! Ker-chug! went the steady push of the machine.

John and the machine drilled without stopping for more than an hour. Chunks of rock flew through the air on both sides. The crowd held its breath. Finally another gunshot was heard, and the men stopped.

John Henry's boss stepped up to look at the holes that had been drilled. He measured each of them. "The machine has sent the drill five feet into the rock," he called.

The man from the city smiled.

"John Henry has sent his drill *six* feet into the rock," cried the boss. The salesman's smile faded. But a cheer rose from the crowd. The people were glad. They didn't want to see a machine beat their John Henry.

The man from the city was angry. He started the steam drill up again.

"Hey, wait for me!" John Henry cried. He started to work again. *Pow! Pow! Pow!* went the hammers. John hit the drill so hard that the heads on both hammers were soon worn out. Someone quickly ran to get new ones.

The machine picked up speed and power. It shook and groaned. It sent thick steam high into the air. *Ka-pow! Ka-pow! Ka-pow!* went the steam drill as it smashed deeper and deeper through the rock.

Now huge stones were flying this way and that. People put their hands in front of their faces to be safe. The very ground shook under their feet.

At last the gun went off again. The boss stepped out and did some careful measuring. "The machine has pushed the drill *ten* feet through the rock," he said. "And John has sent his drill *nine* feet through the rock."

This time there was no shout of joy from the crowd.

John looked at his wife. He smiled and asked her to sing a song for him. "That would make me feel just fine," he said.

There were tears in Polly's eyes. She was frightened, but she started to sing for her husband. Then, one by one, the other people in the camp took up Polly's song. It was about a steel-driving man named John Henry. John thought that his heart would burst with joy. It felt so wonderful to know that all these people cared so much about him.

Then John's hammers went crashing down on his drill a third time. The hammers were singing a song now. *"Win! Win! Win! Win!"* they cried. The steam drill joined in with its own loud song. Never before in any camp had there been such a racket.

John swung his red-hot hammers around and around. Men rushed over to throw pails of cold water on the hammers. This was so the hammers wouldn't just melt away.

The steam drill raced on faster and faster. *Ker-pam! Ker-pam! Ker-pam! Ker-pam!* It tore its way deeper through the rock. The steam drill rattled and puffed, rattled and puffed! It seemed as if it might explode at any moment.

Great rivers of sweat rolled down John Henry's back. The sun felt like a huge, hot fist beating down on him.

"Ha!" cried John. "Not even the sun can stop me. I'll beat this steam drill or die doing it!" John swung his hammers faster than ever before. Bit by bit, the drill sank into the rock. *Bam! Bam! Bam!* went the machine. The drill looked like a nail being pushed into soft clay.

Now John's great hammers could barely be seen as they sped around and around like wheels of fire. Tears rolled down Polly's face as she watched her husband. She clutched tightly at her handkerchief.

The final shot rang through the air. The contest was over! The crowd pushed toward the boss as he measured the holes in the rock. The people held their breath.

It didn't take the boss long to find out who had won the contest. A big smile covered his face. "John Henry is the champion!" he cried. "He's beaten the machine!"

The crowd cheered and danced around John and Polly. There were so many people around them that John and Polly were hidden from sight. The crowd cheered on and on for their hero.

But all at once the cheering stopped. The people grew still. Everything was very, very quiet. All that could be heard was the sound of Polly's sobbing.

John Henry, the mighty steel-driver, was dead! He had worked with every ounce of strength in his body to win for the people who believed in him. But the strain had been too much for his great heart. With the final blow of the hammer, it had burst apart in his chest. Yet he *had* won. And those who saw him on that day said that John Henry, the champion, had fallen with a smile on his lips.

CASEY JONES, HERO
OF THE FLAMING RAILS

engineer [*en je NIR*]—a person who makes an engine go; a man who drives a train

The *engineer* made his train go speeding over the rails.

foreman [*FOR man*]—a man in charge of a group of workers

The *foreman* asked the men to work a little faster.

locomotive [*lo kuh MO tiv*]—the railroad engine car that pulls the rest of the train

The engineer rides in the cabin of the *locomotive*.

prompt [*PROMPT*]—on time

George was *prompt* in getting to school each morning.

shrill [*SHRILL*]—high-pitched or sharp

The motor made a *shrill* noise.

switch [*SWICH*]—to move or change from one thing to another

John was asked to *switch* from one seat to another.

Many signals are used to warn people of danger. In schools, students know the signals used to warn them of fire or other dangers. What signals are used in your school?

Here is a short list of signals. Do you know which danger each of them warns about? You may have more than one answer for some of them.

A lantern in the road
A siren
A honking horn
A flashing light
A loud bell

Can you think of any other danger warnings?

In this story you will learn about some signals that were used on a night in 1900. That was the night Casey Jones proved himself to be a great American hero.

Hel-loo-oo-oo! The shrill voice sang through the night. People smiled when they heard the whistle on the locomotive. They knew that only engineer Casey Jones could make the whistle speak like that.

Sam Howard was sitting on his front steps. "There goes the eight-thirty train," he said. "Hm, guess my watch is a bit slow. I'd better fix it."

Yessir! Casey's Cannonball Express was always on time. It was so prompt that people could set their clocks by it.

This evening, Casey gave the whistle one more toot. Then he pulled his train into the railroad yard. When the train stopped, he and his fireman, Sim Webb, jumped off. Laughing and talking, they went into the yard office.

They stopped laughing when they saw how upset the foreman was. "Why are you looking so worried?" Casey asked. "What's wrong?"

"Plenty!" groaned the foreman. "The engineer of Train 638 is sick. He can't bring his train in, and we need the supplies his train is carrying."

Casey took off his cap and spun it around on his hand. Then he looked at Sim, and Sim looked at Casey. The fireman knew what was on his friend's mind. Sim laughed out loud. "All right, pal," Sim grinned. "If you really want to."

Casey's gray eyes twinkled. He pulled his striped cap down on his head. "Stop worrying," he told the foreman. "We'll go back and pull in old Number 638!"

The foreman knew how tired the two men were. He wanted to turn down their offer, but he knew they wouldn't take no for an answer. So, ten minutes later, the Cannonball was speeding along the tracks once more. *Hel-loo-oo-oo!* The whistle sang again through the night.

There was just one star in the sky. Casey looked up at it. Then he pulled on the whistle cord. "Twinkle, twinkle, little star," sang the whistle. Casey did it to make Sim laugh. And Sim did laugh, for a moment.

Then he pointed to the sky. "Did you see that?" he asked.

Casey looked again at the dark sky. "I don't see anything," he said. "What's wrong, Sim? Seeing things?"

"No," said the fireman. "I'm not joking now." Sim's eyes searched the sky. Suddenly he exclaimed, "There it is again! A strange light!"

This time Casey saw it too. "It looks like a signal rocket," said Casey.

"You're right," answered Sim. "That's just what it is!"

Casey and Sim looked at each other. All trainmen used

rockets to warn of danger or trouble. The two knew one thing for sure. A train was in trouble out there in the night.

Yes, somewhere in the darkness a train had switched to the wrong track. Now its engineer was trying to warn other trains that might be racing through the night toward it. Of course, Casey and Sim didn't know just what was wrong. They knew only that a train was in real trouble, somewhere.

Casey and Sim leaned out of the cabin. They were trying to see through the darkness. "Can't see a thing," mumbled Casey. The Cannonball was still racing down the tracks.

Suddenly Casey had an idea. Pulling on the whistle cord, he started to send out signals. He wanted everyone to know the Cannonball was not far off.

Hel-loo-oo-oo! Hel-loo-oo-oo! The whistle kept singing over and over. The Cannonball sped on through the night. Sim put his hand to his ear. "Hear that?" cried Sim at last. "Do you hear that?"

Casey listened hard. He could hear a whistle answering his. "It's not far off," Casey called. "And it's getting louder and louder."

Sim and Casey shook their heads. They were afraid of what the other whistle might mean. "Do you think there's a train on our track?" Sim whispered.

Casey didn't answer. He was thinking hard. "What's on your mind?" Sim asked at last.

Casey said, "You'll find out soon enough."

The Cannonball zoomed through the night. Sparks flew from between the wheels and the tracks. Casey looked at the sparks. He thought the train was going too fast. He cut the speed a little, just in case they might have to come to a quick stop. The Cannonball went around a bend and started down a steep hill.

Near the foot of the hill was a second set of rails. These rails ran right across the track the Cannonball was on.

Suddenly a red rocket burst in the sky. Casey and Sim stared at it. They knew it could mean only one thing. A train was coming along on the other track, and it was headed right for them!

"How can that be?" cried Sim. "No train should be on those rails at this hour. What's it doing there?"

Casey reached for the brakes. "That must be the train in trouble. It must have switched onto the wrong track," he cried. Then he tugged on the whistle cord. If only he could warn the other train to slow down! Trying to see through the darkness, he and Sim leaned out of the cabin. Fear shone in their eyes.

The men saw a beam of light flash across the other track. "There *is* a train on those rails," cried Casey. "And it doesn't look as if it can pass us in time!"

The two men looked at each other. "Jump!" Casey shouted to Sim. "Jump, I tell you!"

Sim didn't obey the order. He was going to stay on the Cannonball with his friend.

"Jump, Sim! Please!" Casey cried once more. "We may hit the other train!"

It was almost useless by this time, but Casey tugged with all his might at the brakes. Sim tugged with him. All of a sudden, Casey gave Sim a push. It sent him sailing right off the train. Sim went rolling over and over down the hill.

Now Casey pulled the whistle cord again. He was trying to warn the men on the other train to jump off. Could he do it? Was there still time? With all his might he pulled on the cord and held it down. The whistle screamed a last, long warning.

The men on the other train heard the whistle. Looking up, they saw the Cannonball racing down the hill toward them. They could hear the screeching wheels! They could see the sparks shooting from the tracks!

"Jump!" screamed the men to each other. "Jump! Jump!"

The men had just enough time to leap off their train before the crash. A second later, the Cannonball smashed straight into the other train's side. Wheels flew off. Boards flew up. Glass and burning coals went sailing through the night.

Soon the only sound was the hiss of steaming rails and the crackle of fire. Bits of burning wood and coal covered the ground. The men who had been saved stared silently at the wrecked trains.

Then the men stumbled through the smoke and flames to the cabin of the Cannonball. They stared inside, open-mouthed.

"Why, that's Casey Jones in there!" cried the engineer. "He saved our lives! But he gave his own to do it."

The men took off their caps and bowed their heads. They looked sadly at the crumpled figure of Casey lying in the front of the cabin.

"Casey Jones did everything one man can do for another," said the engineer. "And he would have done more if he could. Look there. His hand is still on the whistle cord. . . ."

A GRAB BAG OF TALL
TALES *From the South*

A farmer in West Virginia claims to have had the smartest dog in the land. He said that one night he watched his dog feed lightning bugs to a frog. The dog kept doing this until the frog was filled up and shining with light. The farmer claims that the dog then picked up the frog and carried it around as a lantern.

The tale of the fisher-hound, told in many southern states, tells how a man learned a wonderful new way to fish. It seems that the fisherman wasn't getting a bite, so he became bored. To amuse himself, he threw a silver dollar into the water just to see his dog dive after it. The dog leaped into the water and was gone for ten minutes. When he got back to shore, he was carrying eight pounds of catfish and fifteen cents in change.

In North Carolina, people are still talking about the lady who tried to put sunbeams in a wheelbarrow and carry them into the house to dry her floor.

In Kentucky, they tell about the stupidest mule that ever lived. This mule lived on the southern shore of the Cumberland River. One day the mule's owner took him across the river to do some work. Everything was going along well until the mule plunged into the water and began swimming to the other side. When the mule reached the southern bank, he stepped ashore and turned around. Then he began to take the drink he had forgotten to get before they had left home that morning.

Lake County in Florida has 1400 lakes noted for their big-mouth bass. So many men have been pulled into the water by these fish that the state now makes each man take a physical examination when he asks for a fishing license. He must show that he can at least bulldoze a steer or wrestle a tiger before he can get his license.

Riding West

THE COURAGE
OF "BIRD WOMAN"

amazed   [*uh MAZED*]—surprised
         The class was *amazed* at how well Mary sang.

debt   [*DET*]—something owed
         Robert worked hard for money to pay his *debt*.

guide   [*GIDE*]—person who leads the way
         The men needed a *guide* to take them through the forest.

interpreter [*in TER pret er*]—person who changes a speech from one language into another
         The *interpreter* told the Canadians what the Indian said.

territory [*TAIR i tor ee*]—big stretch of land
         The *territory* was settled by pioneers.

In this book we have read some legends that have grown up around the deeds of Americans who helped to make our land great. But we should not forget the debt we owe to some of the *first* Americans, the Indians of this land.

When the Pilgrims settled in Plymouth, they lived through the first winter only because of Squanto, their Indian friend. He showed the men how to hunt, fish, and plant corn. He was their guide, and he helped to keep peace between the Pilgrims and his Indian brothers. Squanto was a great Indian hero of the East.

This is a story about a famous Indian heroine of the West. In it, you will learn how young, pretty Sacajawea risked her safety and her future, just to keep a promise to her friends.

Dawn was coming up over the little village in North Dakota. Meriwether Lewis, the great explorer, walked up and down in front of the cabin in which he was spending the winter months. His fellow explorer William Clark pulled on his long leather boots and hurried outside to join him.

"Are they in sight yet?" asked Clark.

Lewis shook his head. "No, but the Frenchman promised he'd have a guide here by this morning. If he doesn't, we'll have to spend the rest of the winter trying to find one of our own."

Lewis and Clark had already come a long way on their journey West. Their project had begun in 1803, when President Thomas Jefferson bought the Louisiana Territory from France. The Territory stretched from the Mississippi River all the way to the Rocky Mountains. The President had sent Lewis and Clark to lead a party to explore the western wilderness. So the pair had traveled down the Ohio River, up the Mississippi and then up the Missouri for hundreds of miles. But the President wanted Lewis and Clark to go even farther. He wanted them to explore the country all the way to the shores of the Pacific Ocean! It was a trip that would take about two years to complete.

Of course, they needed a guide to explore this strange country. That was why they were waiting for the Frenchman. Actually, he was a French Canadian named Charbonneau [*Shar bon NO*]. He had come from Canada to live and work among the Indians. He had learned their language and taken an Indian wife. He had become an interpreter between the Indians and the traders of the Northwest Fur Company. After meeting Lewis and Clark, Charbonneau promised to find an Indian guide for them.

Now the two explorers watched eagerly in front of their log cabin for the Frenchman. They could see the path he would take to reach them.

"At last!" Clark said. "There he is. But where is the guide? There's no one with him but his wife."

When the pair came up to the cabin, Lewis asked impatiently, "Well, have you found us a guide?"

"Of course," answered the Frenchman. "And the one I've picked to travel with us even speaks the Shoshone [*Sho SHO nee*] language. We've got to go through Shoshone country, you know."

"Wonderful," said Lewis, "but where is he?"

"The guide I've brought you knows every hill, stream and path leading into the Shoshone country. She has a fine memory."

"*She?*" asked Lewis. "Did you say *she?*"

"Yes," said the Frenchman. "Your guide is to be my

162

wife, Sacajawea [*Sa ka ja WEE ah*]. Her name means 'Bird Woman.' "

The explorers stared at the small, pretty girl. She seemed no more than seventeen years old. She had long, shining black hair, and her dark eyes sparkled.

"But that's impossible," said Lewis. "This is no trip for a woman. We've got to cross dangerous rivers and steep mountains. And the Indians we meet may not be friendly."

The Frenchman shrugged. "Sacajawea is the only one in this area who speaks Shoshone," he said. "You see, my wife is really a Shoshone. She was taken from her village about seven years ago by a war party from another tribe. They took her to their village. That's where I met and married her."

Lewis didn't know what to say. He was against taking a woman on such a dangerous trip. But he needed a guide badly, and here was one who even spoke the Shoshone language. Finally he gave in.

And so, that winter, Sacajawea became Lewis and Clark's guide. She spent the next few months giving them advice on which supplies should be packed. She also directed the men as they fixed up the many boats that would be needed.

Then, one warm morning in April, Lewis and Clark were ready to start out. With her infant son strapped to her back, Sacajawea stepped into the first canoe of the exploring party. Her husband and the two explorers sat with her. Soon the party of forty people, loaded in ten boats, started out.

At first some of the men in the party weren't happy about having Sacajawea as their guide. "A girl for guide?" muttered one man. "Even though she is a Shoshone, what can she remember about this land? She hasn't seen it since she was a child." But he and the others were soon to learn how lucky they were.

163

From the beginning, Sacajawea kept watch carefully. She knew that if the boats took a wrong turn on the river the whole party could be lost or go crashing over the waterfalls.

Time and time again, she amazed the men with her wonderful memory. Once she said, "There should be a great rock shaped like a beaver about three hours' ride from here." Sure enough, at the end of the three hours, the great rock rose into view. After that, the men trusted her every word.

Weeks went by. The men were tired, but they weren't unhappy or afraid. Sacajawea's smiling face and lovely songs filled their hearts with courage.

Early one morning, the boats went around a sharp bend in the river. Sacajawea's smile lit up her whole face. "We are here," she cried. "This is the land of the Shoshone nation. This is the land of my people." The men could see that there were tears in her eyes.

Sacajawea was right again. Soon the banks were filled with hundreds of Shoshone Indians.

"They outnumber us fifty to one," said one of the men in the boats. "It would be easy for them to make short work of us and take everything we have." But he soon learned that the Indians meant no harm.

The Shoshones were expecting the visitors. Indian lookouts had been watching the ten boats move up the river for two days. The Indians made signs to show the explorers that they were welcome to come ashore.

When the boats reached the land, the Indians led the exploring party to a big hut. The chiefs of all the Shoshone villages had gathered in it for a meeting. The Indian braves allowed Lewis and Clark to go into the hut, but Sacajawea and the others waited outside.

When they went in, the explorers saw the great chief of

the Shoshones sitting on a white robe. There were bright shells in his long dark hair. His shirt was covered with beads and feathers of many colors.

Smoking his pipe, the great chief nodded to the explorers. In sign language, he told the men to sit down on the furs that had been brought for them.

Lewis made signs to tell the chief that there was someone outside who could speak the Shoshone language. The chief understood and nodded to Lewis.

"Send in our guide," Lewis called. "Send in the woman."

The bearskin curtain was pulled aside. Sacajawea stepped into the hut. With her child in her arms, she stood there with her eyes fixed on the ground. She was waiting for the great chief to speak first.

"Come forward," said the chief in the Shoshone language.

As Sacajawea walked toward the chief, she raised her eyes. When she saw the chief's face, her eyes flashed brightly. Could this be real? Or was it a dream?

Running to the chief, she cried, "Brother! My brother! Don't you know me? I'm the sister who was taken away many years ago. I am Sacajawea! And this is my son!"

The chief stared at her and the child for a few seconds. Then, smiling, he reached out and took her hand in his.

"Little sister," he said over and over again. "Little sister."

Tears rolled down Sacajawea's face. "Where is our father?" she asked. "If I remember well, the village where he is chief isn't far from here."

The great chief sadly shook his head. "Our father is no longer living," he said. "I became chief of the village after he died. Later, the chiefs of the villages chose me to be the leader of the Shoshone nation."

Lewis and Clark didn't know what the chief and Sacajawea

were saying, but they knew it must be important. Later that day they found out that their little friend and guide was truly an Indian princess.

They watched as the chief pointed to a child in the arms of an old woman. "That is the child of our oldest sister," he said. "She died last spring, leaving the baby without a mother."

Sacajawea looked at the sleeping baby. "Brother, great chief," she said, "let me adopt this child as my own. I will raise him as a brother to my own son."

"It shall be as you wish, little sister," said the chief. "Now sit here beside me, and tell me who these people are. Why have you brought them here?"

First Sacajawea called her husband inside to meet the chief. Then she explained that Lewis and Clark were trying to reach the water that is always salty. She said that the men were her friends. She said that they needed horses and supplies in order to continue on their way.

The chief was glad to help. He had his braves bring horses to trade for the things the explorers had to offer.

Lewis and Clark enjoyed the weeks they spent with the Shoshones. In fact, Lewis wrote the following words in the log he kept of the journey: "The Indians are men of honor. They do not try to bother us, though they outnumber us greatly. The honesty of our Indian friends is wonderful. They return even the smallest tools they borrow from us."

Finally it was time to leave. Lewis sent a messenger to ask the chief for some guides, for he thought that Sacajawea would want to remain with her people. But when she heard of this, she ran to the chief. "Brother," she said, "I am their guide. I have promised to go with them."

The chief looked at her. "But you can stay here and have the honor that is yours as a princess of the Shoshone nation. If you go, think of the great dangers you will have to face in the mountains and beyond."

Sacajawea shook her head. "I would not be a true Shoshone if I did not keep my promise," she said. "I have given my word to lead my friends to the water that is always salty."

The chief's heart swelled with pride to hear her words. He turned and looked at his braves. He could see how they admired their brave princess.

Sacajawea said she would be back for her sister's child. Then, climbing back into the canoe, she led the Lewis and Clark party forward. They pushed ahead, sometimes on land and sometimes on water. As they went along, Lewis kept a record of the plant and animal life he saw.

The explorers reached the place where the Missouri River begins. Then the party of brave men started its trip over the Rocky Mountains. Over great rocks and through narrow passes Sacajawea led the men. Again she filled the men's hearts with courage as they saw how tireless she was. They knew that if she hadn't been with them, they would surely have died in the mountains. They listened to every word of advice she gave them. And they gladly took the medicine she made from roots when some of them were sick.

Finally, Sacajawea led the party along a stream that grew wider and deeper. Soon it turned into a rushing river, now known as the Columbia. Sometimes the water ran so rough and fast that it seemed to be boiling foam. But the men felt no fear. Sacajawea was there, smiling and pointing out the way.

One morning she announced, "Soon we will see the water

that is always salty." Less than an hour later, the men could see the place where the Columbia River runs into the Pacific Ocean.

The men looked at their Indian guide. Proudly she stood on the shore, her long hair flying in the ocean breeze. Her eyes shone with the excitement of the great adventure they had been through. "Truly, this is a princess," they thought, "a noble girl whose name will never be forgotten."

And those men were right. Sacajawea returned safely to her people and adopted her sister's child. Soon after, a river was named for her by Meriwether Lewis. A mountain pass in Montana was also given her name. But most of all, Sacajawea's name has lived on in the hearts of all Americans who admire great courage.

DAVY CROCKETT AND
HIS FELLOW HEROES
OF THE ALAMO

Vocabulary Preview

colonel — [*KER nel*]—officer in the army
The *colonel* led his troops into battle.

independence — [*in de PEN dens*]—freedom from the rule of others
The United States declared its *independence* from England in 1776.

mission — [*MISH in*]—place where holy men and women help people and teach them about religion
Walls were sometimes built around *missions* to keep the buildings and people safe from harm.

ordinary — [*OR din air ee*]—plain, common, usual
She wore an *ordinary* hat to the show.

republic — [*re PUB lik*]—a nation in which the people choose their own rulers
Texas was once a *republic*.

terror — [*TAIR or*]—very great fear
The people were filled with *terror* when the ground began to shake.

Geronimo! This was the cry of American parachute troops during the Second World War. The troops would shout the name of the daring Indian chief just before leaping from their high-flying planes. Why do you suppose the men chose this name as their battle cry?

Another famous cry you may have heard is *Don't give up the ship!* What is the story behind this battle cry?

As you read this story you will learn about a group of truly great heroes—and the first use of another famous battle cry.

"WELL, BOYS, THERE IT IS," said Davy Crockett. Just ahead lay San Antonio, in the Mexican territory of Texas.

"And just beyond those walls is the Alamo, the old mission that's now a fort. That's where we're to fight Santa Anna. And that's where we'll win Texas' freedom!"

"I hope we're not too late," said Bee-hunter, one of the four friends traveling with Davy. Bee-hunter was a happy young man who was forever singing about his sweetheart Kate. He had gotten his strange name because he often followed bees to find the honey he loved to eat.

Davy grinned at Bee-hunter. "Too late? I don't think so. If Santa Anna's men were here, you'd know it. But they will be, so come on! Let's get to the fort."

The men raced their horses toward the town. As they rode along, Davy thought of his wife and children. He had left them back in Tennessee.

Davy's family had understood how he felt about wanting to help the people of Texas win their freedom. But they had hated to see him go. They had said good-by with smiles on their faces and sadness in their hearts. For they wondered if they would ever see him again.

Davy and his friends rode through the town of San Antonio. It was just a village at that time. In 1836, Texas was still a part of Mexico. But many Americans felt that the territory really belonged to the United States. They felt it was part of the land that France had sold to America in 1803. Besides, more than three-fourths of the settlers in Texas were Americans.

Santa Anna was the president of Mexico. He was trying to stop more Americans from coming to Texas to live. The Americans who were already there didn't like this. They thought it was time to declare their independence from Mexico. And one of the great battles to help them win that independence was soon to take place at the Alamo.

Davy and his friends gave their names to the guard at the gate and went inside the fort. The men in the fort cheered when they saw that the famous Davy Crockett had come to help them. Colonel Travis, who was in charge of the fort, came out to shake hands with Davy and his friends.

Then Jim Bowie hurried over. "Burn my boots if it isn't Davy Crockett himself!" shouted Jim. "We can't lose now, I tell you!"

Davy laughed. "Keep quiet, partner," he said. "Shut your mouth or your teeth'll get sunburned."

But Jim was not to be stopped. He whistled and clapped while the men lifted Davy to their shoulders and carried him around. When they put Davy down, Jim cried, "We'll beat Santa Anna's troops for sure. And if bullets don't bring them down, *this* will!" He waved his great knife in the air. It was the famous bowie knife that he had invented.

When the cheering died down, everyone could hear Jim coughing. He was coughing so hard that he could hardly catch his breath.

"I don't like the sound of that," said Colonel Travis. "Jim, you'd better go inside and get into bed."

"Oh, I'm all right," answered Jim.

"You're to go to bed, and that's an order," shouted Travis. "I want you well before Santa Anna's men get here. We need you, Jim."

Jim grinned like a boy. Then he turned to go. "See you later, Davy," he called as he went off. But Jim was much sicker than he knew. There was something wrong with his lungs.

Travis turned to Davy. "Glad you're with us," he said. "With you and your friends here, we now have one hundred and eighty-seven men."

"Is that all?" asked Davy.

Travis nodded. "Yes," he sighed. "And I've heard reports that more than sixteen hundred of Santa Anna's men are on their way here."

Davy let out a low whistle. "Why, he's sending a whole army," he said. "Why is he sending so many men to capture this one little fort?"

Colonel Travis led Davy and his friends to the kitchen to get them something to eat. "This is no ordinary fort to Santa Anna," said Travis. "Ever since it was taken from his men last December, Santa Anna has been saying that he means to take it back. I guess he's ashamed that a small band of Texans could take a fort away from his armed troops. Besides, he means to punish all Texans who refuse to be ruled by Mexico."

"But we'll talk about Santa Anna later. Now it's time for you to eat and rest," said Travis. Then he left the kitchen and went back to his office to work.

The days passed slowly that February, and everything seemed as peaceful as ever. Then one afternoon, Davy and his friends were spending a few hours in town. Suddenly a man on horseback galloped wildly toward them.

"What's the hurry?" called Davy.

"Santa Anna's men are two miles away!" shouted the rider. "And Santa Anna is leading them himself!" Then he turned and dashed off to the fort.

Davy and his friends rode back to the Alamo at once. The townspeople hurried after them. They could already hear the bugle blowing and the drums beating inside the fort.

The Texans were ready to fight, but Santa Anna's men didn't appear that day. The next morning at dawn, however, hundreds and hundreds of Mexican soldiers could be seen moving toward the town. The people in the Alamo watched from the windows and the tops of the walls.

That morning, Davy Crockett wrote in his diary: "Early this morning the enemy came in sight. They were marching to show us their great strength. They hoped to fill us with terror. But that was no use. They'll find out that they have to deal with men who will never lay down their arms as long as they can stand on their legs."

The flag of the Republic of Texas was flying over the Alamo. The flag had a red and a white stripe on it. In the corner, against a blue background, was one big, white star.

The sight of this flag made Santa Anna angry. He sent his men to take the town of San Antonio. Then he ordered them to send up a red flag over the town. This flag seemed to be a warning of the blood that would be lost if the people in the Alamo put up a fight.

Santa Anna then sent a messenger to the front gate of the Alamo. Davy and Colonel Travis looked down at the messenger from a window.

"What do you want?" called Travis.

"The great Santa Anna gives you one chance to save yourselves," shouted the messenger. "You must surrender the Alamo and promise to obey the laws of Mexico!"

The answer came right away: BOOM! A burst of cannon shot sent the dust flying up in front of the messenger's horse. The soldier wheeled his horse around and galloped quickly back to Santa Anna.

At once, the angry president ordered his men to begin firing on the Alamo. The heavy shelling continued for many days. Travis knew that the people in the Alamo couldn't hold out long against Santa Anna's army, so he called for his scouts.

"One of you must try to get to the nearest fort," Travis told them. "Tell the Texans there that we will surely all be killed if we don't get help soon."

"I'll go," said a scout everyone called Old Pirate. "But I'll come back if I can't get through Santa Anna's lines. I'll start out tonight after dark."

Colonel Travis then called the rest of his men together. "If any of you want to leave," he told them, "now is the time. We're in grave trouble, and we can't count on help from outside."

When no one moved, he went on. "If you stay, I ask one thing—that each of you fight to the last breath. There will be no surrender! What do you say?"

For a moment the men were silent. Then, all together, they

began to cheer. Their courage filled the colonel's heart with both joy and sorrow.

Each day after that, the men of the Alamo watched from the shell-torn walls to see if any help was in sight. But day after day, all they saw were more and more men arriving to join Santa Anna. Soon the Mexican army numbered more than five thousand men.

Then one day, while he was watching from the wall, Bee-hunter shouted to Davy, "Look over there! Someone's running toward the fort. It looks like Old Pirate!"

Five soldiers were chasing Old Pirate toward the fort. Davy and Bee-hunter didn't waste any time. They rushed out of the fort to help their friend. All at once Old Pirate stopped running. He spun quickly around and started firing at the soldiers. Then he began to run toward them. Santa Anna's men were so surprised that they turned and ran for their lives.

Just then, Davy and Bee-hunter reached Old Pirate. They grabbed him by the arms and started to run back to the fort. As they ran, a group of soldiers on horseback galloped ahead and blocked their way to the Alamo. Davy and his friends didn't stop to think of the danger. Guns blazing, they rushed straight toward the soldiers.

By this time, several others had run out of the Alamo to help Davy and his friends. Their bullets brought down one of Santa Anna's men. The others soon turned and scattered. Finally, Davy and his friends were inside the fort.

Davy was now safe, but he was very sad. Old Pirate had been shot in the back. When they got inside, he fell dead at Davy's feet. To add to Davy's sorrow, Bee-hunter sank to the ground. There was a bullet hole in his chest.

Davy carried Bee-hunter to a bed and tried to dress the

terrible wound. Colonel Travis hurried in to see what he could do. But when he saw Bee-hunter, he shook his head sadly. Davy knew his friend wouldn't live through the night.

Bee-hunter had a little smile on his face. He didn't seem to know where he was. He smiled and sang softly to himself about his home and about Kate, the sweetheart he'd never see again.

By midnight, Bee-hunter was gone. "Poor Kate," said Davy. "Who will tell her?" Then Davy got to his feet and went to stand at the top of the wall. Everyone left him alone that night.

The fighting began again at dawn. It went on all through the morning. Davy took only a moment to write this in his diary: "Boom, boom, boom, all through the day! No time for writing now. Go ahead! Liberty and independence forever!"

That night, after the fighting had stopped, Davy went in to see Jim Bowie. Jim was still in bed, looking very tired and weak.

"I want to get up and fight," said Jim, "but my legs won't carry me."

"Take it easy," said Davy. "When you're feeling better you can do your share of fighting."

Jim was silent. Then he sighed. "I wonder when their *big* attack will come," he said. He closed his eyes.

Just before dawn on the morning of March 6, the whole Mexican army attacked the Alamo at once. The big attack had come. Shouts and screams filled the air. Cannons roared. Bullets whistled everywhere. Men fell from their horses and dropped from the walls of the fort.

Thick smoke, horses without riders, wounded men—confusion was everywhere. Cannonballs tore holes in the sides of the fort. Santa Anna's men climbed in through the windows and over the walls. They searched every corner, shooting anyone they found.

Soon they came to the room where Jim Bowie lay. He sat up in bed, his guns ready, when the soldiers charged into his room. Firing away, he brought down two of them. The others ran back to take cover in the doorway. But they couldn't get away from Jim. He fired until his bullets were gone. Then he threw away his empty guns and reached for his famous knife. Throwing it, he brought down still another of the enemy.

But finally, his weapons gone and his body weak, Jim was helpless. Carefully one of the soldiers took aim from behind the door, and put a bullet through the heart of the great fighter.

Outside, the battle was still going on. Davy Crockett could be seen here and there through the smoke. He seemed to be everywhere at once—shooting at Mexicans, handing bullets to his friends, shoving an enemy through a window, shouting praise to the Indian warrior who had come to help the Texans. "Go ahead!" he kept yelling through it all. "Freedom for Texas! Liberty forever!"

The battle of the Alamo raged on until daylight. When the first rays of the sun appeared, all but six of the brave heroes were dead. Those six had been captured. One of the men who had been taken prisoner was Davy Crockett. His clothing was torn and covered with dust. He was breathing hard. Blood from a sword cut streamed down from his forehead.

Davy and his friends were now the prisoners of General Castillon. The general was a brave man, but he was not cruel. He didn't want any more men to be killed. He hoped to save Davy and the others by speaking to Santa Anna.

178

"Why do you bring them to me?" shouted the cruel Santa Anna, as he stood in the yard of the fort. "I told you what to do with all who fight against my rule." Then he raised his arm. About thirty soldiers, their swords drawn, ran toward Davy and the other prisoners.

Davy let out a fearful yell and leaped forward. "I promised to fight to the death, and I will," he shouted. Davy swung his mighty fist and knocked down one soldier. Then, as the men came at him, he knocked over two more. He fought like a tiger, but it was no use. Davy Crockett soon fell, without a groan, run through by more than a dozen swords.

But Davy Crockett's story does not really end here. Neither does the story of Texas' fight for freedom. For when the people of Texas heard of the death of Davy, Jim Bowie and the other heroes at the Alamo, they swept like a storm over Santa Anna's army.

"Remember the Alamo! Remember the Alamo!" they shouted as they beat Santa Anna's men in battle after battle. With that famous cry, they finally captured the proud Santa Anna himself at the battle of San Jacinto.

Texas became an independent republic, with Sam Houston as its first president. In 1845, nine years after the battle of the Alamo, Texas became the twenty-eighth state to join the United States of America. And all Americans know that this could never have happened if it hadn't been for men like Davy Crockett and his fellow heroes of the Alamo.

ANNIE OAKLEY,
CHAMPION SHARPSHOOTER

Vocabulary Preview

assistant   [*uh* SIS *tunt*]—a helper
           The doctor's *assistant* cut the bandage.
entertainer   [*en tur* TA *nur*]—a performer, a person who amuses others
           The *entertainer* performed card tricks.
manager   [MAN *eh jur*]—a person in charge, someone who carries on business affairs for others
           The *manager* of the team wanted to set up another game.
sharpshooter   [SHARP *shoo tur*]—a person skilled at shooting, especially with a rifle
           Buffalo Bill was a *sharpshooter* who could hit any target.

Phoebe Ann Oakley Mozee was known as Annie Oakley throughout the world. She was a famous entertainer and perhaps the greatest sharpshooter that ever lived. Even as a child she was a dead shot. And in five years she paid off the mortgage on the family farm with earnings on the game she shot. Her fame as a crack shot quickly spread.

In 1870 GROWNUPS smiled as they watched Annie Oakley carrying quail and other birds into town to sell. "That's how she helps support her family," said one man to his friends. "And it wouldn't surprise me if that ten year old crack shot turns out to be a greater sharpshooter than Buffalo Bill!"

The years rolled by, and Annie was a teen-ager when she heard that Frank Butler, the great sharpshooter was challenging others to a shooting match. "I'm scared to meet him," Annie told her folks, "but we sure can use the prize money. I've got to give it a try."

On the day of the match Annie noticed a blue-eyed man staring at her. She blushed when she learned the handsome fellow was Frank Butler. Annie felt like running away, but before she knew it the contest had begun.

She saw that Frank was a real champion. His bullets easily shattered the clay discs, called clay pigeons, as they were thrown into the air. But much to everyone's surprise, Annie was able to match his record shot for shot.

Then Frank aimed at his last target, pulled the trigger—and *missed!* People gasped. Then they turned to watch Annie as she fired her last shot, and they cheered when the clay pigeon shattered into bits. Annie was the winner!

She quickly turned her head so that her long wavy hair hid part of her face from Frank. But he rushed over and said, "You're great, Annie. You should be on the stage."

Annie just lowered her eyes. "Listen," Frank went on, "think about the places you can visit. And think about the money you can send home."

The sharpshooter did think about these things—but mostly about Frank. And before she was sixteen years old, she was married to the charming Irishman. Two years later she was appearing as the star of a shooting act, with Frank as manager and assistant.

People came from far and wide to see Annie perform. They enjoyed watching her shatter glass balls thrown high into the air, one after the other. And they loved it when she shot down as many as five or six thrown into the air at one time.—Another trick they enjoyed was when she shot down a ball on a string being swung around in the air by Frank. Annie made it extra hard for herself by sighting the moving ball in a mirror.

The first time she did this trick the crowd cheered wildly. And after the show tears came to her eyes as she held one of the many love poems that Frank wrote for her through the years.

They were very happy, and one day in 1885 they were made even happier when Buffalo Bill welcomed Annie and Frank as members of his own great show. His actors were real cowboys, Mexican vaqueros, and Indians—including Chief Sitting Bull himself. These people thrilled audiences as they rode across the show grounds acting out exciting scenes from the history of the West.

And soon the crowds were filled with more excitement as

they watched Annie dressed in buckskin and wearing a cowboy hat come running or riding into view. They clapped loudly as she shot down target after target hurled into the air by cowboys on horseback. And then the audience would grow very, very still as they watched Annie put her rifle on the ground, walk back more than fifty feet, and just stand there without moving. Then, when a target was thrown up, the audience cheered as Annie dashed forward, picked up her gun and shot the target before it reached the ground. To make it harder, she sometimes jumped over a table placed between her and the gun. The amazed people would leap to their feet and scream, "Hurrah for Little Missy, the girl of the golden West!"

People all over America and Europe greatly admired this entertainer. Even kings and queens who saw the show praised her, and some of them sent her medals and other presents.

Annie was a true star, even when she was ill she went on with the show for the sake of her fellow actors and for the people who had come there to be entertained. Among the people she truly loved to entertain were the orphans admitted free on each "Annie Oakley Day" in the cities the show visited.

Things kept on going well. But in 1901, when Annie was still a big star, something terrible happened. As the train carrying Buffalo Bill's show was racing through the night, it crashed head on into another train. Some people were killed, and many show horses had to be destroyed.

"Sweetheart!" Frank shouted as he pulled Annie from the wreck. She was seriously hurt, and before morning her brown hair had turned completely white. The doctors said she might never walk or shoot a gun again.

But Frank and Annie refused to believe this. For two years Frank worked hard to help his wife get stronger. And one day tears streamed down their faces as Annie stood up, raised a rifle, and shattered a clay pigeon as smartly as she had done on the day she and Frank first met.

Annie and Frank were no longer young, but this didn't stop them from helping when World War I broke out. Annie said, "Let's do everything we can to help." Soon she and Frank were putting on shows in army camps around America. It's said that Annie even taught some soldiers a few sharpshooting tricks. And, besides all this, Annie and Frank helped raise money for the Red Cross.

People all over truly admired this wonderful couple. And when Annie died in 1926, many felt that they had lost a dear friend. But the person who felt the loss most was Frank. It's said that he couldn't live without his beloved Annie, and that is why he followed her in death in just a matter of days. Now side by side stand the tombstones, just as Annie and Frank would have wished, of these two sharpshooters and sweethearts —a poet and his girl of the golden West.

THE BATTLE OF THE
TWO GREAT WARRIORS

glory   [*GLOR ee*]—honor; praise
The boys on the team won *glory* for themselves.

mounted   [*MOWN ted*]—climbed up
The cowboy *mounted* his horse and rode away.

regiment   [*REJ i ment*]—large group of soldiers
The *regiment* got ready for the long march.

victory   [*VIK tor ee*]—success; defeat of an enemy
The men hoped for *victory* as the fight began.

188

When we think of battle heroes, we usually think of men like John Paul Jones, Davy Crockett, General Grant and General Douglas MacArthur. As a matter of fact, General MacArthur was sometimes called the "Old Warrior."

American history also includes the names of famous Indian warriors. Have you ever heard of Chief Sitting Bull, Crazy Horse or Rain-in-the-Face?

The story you are about to read tells of a battle between two great fighters. One of them was an American general. The other was a famous Indian leader. No one knows for sure what took place during the last few moments of the fight. But this story is one of the legends that have grown up around that battle.

GEORGE ARMSTRONG CUSTER pinned the shining silver star of his general's rank to the red scarf of his uniform. He stood by the window, waiting eagerly for his scout to return. The general wondered what news the soldier would bring.

Suddenly the Army scout rode into view. The general ran to the door as the scout saluted and leaped from his horse. "Well?" Custer called impatiently. "What did you see?"

"Indians, sir!" the scout answered. "Sioux [SOO] Indians, led by Sitting Bull." He walked toward the cabin. "They're camped along Little Big Horn River, and they're wearing full war paint."

The general had expected this news. There were thousands of Indians in the Dakotas in 1876. And many of them wanted war with the soldiers of the U.S. Army.

"How many of them are there?" Custer asked.

"Not many so far, sir," replied the scout. "We outnumber them."

General Custer stood silently for a moment. Then he turned and went outside. "Bugler!" he cried. "Call the men together!"

When all the troops had gathered, Custer made this announcement: "Sitting Bull is on the warpath. His braves are camped down by the river. Our scout tells me that we outnumber them, so we're going to attack without delay. You must remember that the Sioux fight hard. But we can beat them if we take them by surprise."

In a short time the regiment was moving toward the Little Big Horn. The horses kicked up clouds of yellow dust as the men rode single file across the plains of Montana.

As they drew closer to the Indian camp, the general divided the regiment into three groups. He sent one group toward one side of the camp and another group toward the other side. He planned to lead the third group himself. In this way, he would attack the camp from three sides at once.

Custer waited for a full half hour. Then he looked at his watch. "The other groups should be in place by now," he called. Then the general sat up tall in his saddle and raised his arm above his head. A bugle sounded, and the attack was on! Leading the 264 men in his group, Custer rode full speed toward the Indian camp. With rifles blazing, Custer's men rushed forward to meet the Indians.

At first it seemed as if Custer and his men would have an easy victory. But as he looked around, the general couldn't see the rest of his regiment. He wondered what could be holding them up. Then he looked up at the top of a hill, and a shock passed through his body.

The hilltop was covered with hundreds and hundreds of Sioux warriors on horseback. At their head was the great

Chief Sitting Bull. Their painted faces and bright feathers blazed with color. It was a frightening sight!

Custer turned to look at the opposite hill. There he saw hundreds of Cheyenne [*shy EN*] braves waiting for the signal to attack. Their eyes were fixed on their leader, Chief Rain-in-the-Face. He sat tall and proud on his beautiful brown and white horse. Now Custer knew he had fallen into a trap.

A fierce war whoop broke the silence. At that signal, the Indians stormed down the hills and rushed into battle. Rifle shots echoed through the air! Arrows whizzed. Soldiers fell where they stood. Indians tumbled from their horses.

Custer looked quickly to the left and right. The rest of his men were still not to be seen. The general guessed that these men had fallen into traps too.

"Onward, men! Onward!" the general shouted. His brave men obeyed. Some even leaped from their horses and fought hand to hand. The soldiers didn't give up, even when more and more Indians poured down from the hills.

Soon Custer and his men were trapped in a great circle of Indian braves. Throwing his empty gun away, the general leaped from his horse. He pulled out his sword and rushed into the thick of the battle.

Rain-in-the-Face saw Custer and jumped down from his horse too. He pushed his way through the crowds of fighting men, for he wanted to meet the famous general face to face.

It was an Indian belief that to bring down a great man with bullets didn't count as a true victory. So Rain-in-the-Face threw down his own gun and took out a knife. He would earn glory by killing Custer with a blade.

Now the Indian and Custer were face to face. The two great warriors looked at each other. The moment had come.

Each man turned and dodged to escape the flashing steel of the other. Dust flew as the men lunged at each other and then leaped away. Suddenly, like a wolf, Rain-in-the-Face leaped forward and knocked Custer down. As the general rolled over and over, the Indian jumped back to his feet.

"Now I have you!" cried Rain-in-the-Face. But just then, the few of Custer's soldiers who were left rode between him and their general. Swarms of Indians followed. Now the dust swirled up thicker than ever.

Blinded by clouds of dust, Rain-in-the-Face tried to see what was happening. He could hear gunshots and wild yells as men and horses battled for their lives.

When the dust began to settle, the Indian leader saw Custer. The fight was over for the brave general, and for his men as well. Rain-in-the-Face shook his head sadly. He had wanted to win lasting glory by killing Custer in hand-to-hand combat. Now it was too late. He put away his knife and stared at the body of the fallen hero.

Just then, the Indian brave who had shot Custer ran forward to take the dead man's scalp. But Rain-in-the-Face held up his hand. "Stop!" he cried. "No one must touch the brave warrior general! He was a man who fought with a blade, not with a gun. He was the bravest of his people. He will keep his scalp!"

Then Rain-in-the-Face mounted his horse and called his warriors. He must ride back to meet with Chiefs Crazy Horse and Sitting Bull. They would talk about the victory, and about the way Custer's brave army had fought to the last man.

As the late afternoon sun glittered on the dusty plain, the Indian army rode off. Behind them lay the bodies of George Custer and all his men. And on the general's blood-red scarf, a bright star gleamed like gold beneath the orange sun.

BUFFALO BILL AND THE
HORSE THAT COULD HUNT

dude   [*DOOD*]—cowboy's word for a city-dweller or East-erner
The Eastern *dude* kept falling off his horse.

gallop   [*GAL up*]—run fast, as a horse runs
We saw him *gallop* down the road.

graze   [*GRAZE*]—eat grass that is growing
The cows *graze* in the fields.

lullaby   [*LUL a by*]—song to put a baby to sleep
The mother sang a *lullaby* to the baby.

mustache   [*muss TASH*]—hair growing on a man's upper lip
The man had a red *mustache*.

prairie   [*PRAIR ee*]—large flat land covered with grass
The cowboys rode over the *prairie*.

rudeness   [*ROOD ness*]—not being polite; not having good manners
The boy was not liked because of his *rudeness*.

You have often seen animals perform clever tricks in the movies and on television. Indeed, many of these animals are very good actors. Describe any you have seen recently.

We learn about other clever animals from books we read and from watching animals in real life. Think of the important work being done by seeing-eye dogs and watch dogs. Can you think of any other animals that work for people? What kind of work do they do?

In the following story you will learn about a wonderful horse and his famous master. You will also discover how they proved themselves to be the best team of hunters in the Old West.

IT WAS LATE AFTERNOON. The dudes from the East rode across the prairie, looking for buffalo. So far, they had had no luck. The older of the two, Jim, turned to the other, who was his cousin. "Say, George," he asked. "Are you sure Buffalo Bill killed four thousand buffalo on these plains?"

"Sure, Jim," the young man answered. "*Over* four thousand buffalo! And in less than two years! They were used to feed the railroad workers."

Jim snorted. "Did anyone really *see* him shoot all those buffalo? I think it's a tall tale. In fact, I wish I could meet this Buffalo Bill and take him hunting. I'll bet I could show him a thing or two myself!"

Meanwhile, about a mile away, two hunters had just finished setting up their camp.

"We're all out of meat," said the first hunter. "And I'm so hungry I could eat a whole buffalo, tail and all!"

His partner laughed. "We'll see about that," he said. Then

he jumped up on his horse. "I'll be back in ten shakes of a rattlesnake's tail," he called. "You get a fire going."

"Aren't you going to saddle up?" the first scout called.

"I'm too hungry to waste the time," shouted his partner. Then he whooped like an Indian and rode off.

He hadn't gone very far when he saw the two dudes from the East. The Westerner frowned. He didn't believe men should hunt buffalo just for sport. He believed that buffalo should be hunted only when food was needed.

The dudes saw the stranger eying them. They rode toward him.

"Hey," called Jim. "Did you lose your saddle along the way?" He laughed at his own cleverness. But the stranger didn't answer.

"Your horse looks as if he's ready to fall asleep," Jim called again. "Do you want me to sing him a lullaby?"

The hunter rode up to the men. "My horse *is* tired," he said. "We've been riding hard all day. But Pride will feel better as soon as he spots some buffalo." As he spoke, he patted his horse on the neck.

Jim laughed louder than ever. He stared at the stranger's long hair and mustaches. "I suppose your horse will sniff out the animals," he said, "and then you'll rope them in with those mustaches!"

George was ashamed of his cousin's rudeness. In fact, he couldn't understand why the stranger didn't knock Jim off his horse.

"Say, why don't you come along with us?" laughed Jim. "We'll give you the tails of all the buffalo we shoot!"

George looked at the hunter. "Please don't mind my cousin," he said. "Besides, there aren't any buffalo around here. We've been searching for hours."

The hunter liked the polite young man. But he didn't wait to hear any more. He had already decided to teach that loud-mouth Jim a lesson he'd never forget.

The Westerner shook his horse's reins. "Pride," he whispered, "let's find us some buffalo." Pride began to walk very slowly. He stepped so lightly that his footsteps could barely be heard.

The hunter turned back to the men. "Sh," he said, "don't gallop. Let your horses walk as quietly as a peaceful buffalo."

Soon the men could see why the hunter had said this. Pride led them through a grove of trees and over a hill to a flat stretch of land where thirty or forty buffalo were grazing. The two men were surprised. They brought their horses to a halt and watched to see what would happen next.

The great beasts went on eating quietly. They hadn't heard anything. Pride trotted softly up to a big buffalo at the edge of the herd. Only a few feet away from the beast, Pride stopped. He stood very still. The buffalo hardly noticed him at all. Then the hunter brought his rifle to his shoulder and took aim. He brought down the buffalo with one shot.

When the other buffalo heard the shot, they began to snort and move around. But Pride just walked over to the next animal. The horse stood there quietly while his master took aim. Of course this beast was brought down with a single shot too.

Now all the buffalo knew they were in danger. All together, they dashed off in a cloud of dust. Their pounding hoofs made a noise like thunder.

Pride seemed to come more alive than ever as he ran with the herd. His eyes shone brightly. He started to weave in and out of the herd. He raced and turned and doubled back. His timing was perfect.

Meanwhile, the hunter kept on firing. He didn't even have

to hold the reins. He took care of the shooting, and Pride took care of the rest.

The two men from the East stared with open mouths. They'd never seen anything like that horse. Their own horses had kicked and jumped at the first gunshot. Jim had been thrown to the ground. His fancy hunting jacket was covered with dust.

Jim was still sitting in the dust when the hunter rode up to him. "I've taken the meat for my partner and myself," called the stranger. "Soon my Indian friends will be coming to take the meat I'm leaving behind. But don't worry. I did save something for you!" He threw a buffalo's tail to Jim.

George laughed aloud. "Say, I'd be honored to know your name," he said. "I'll bet you're an even better hunter than Buffalo Bill!"

There was a twinkle in the stranger's eye. "No," he answered. "I'm sure I don't hunt any *better* than Bill. And there's something else I'm sure about."

"What's that?" asked George.

"I'm sure my horse is a better hunter than your cousin," he laughed.

George laughed too. Even his cousin had to grin from his seat in the dust.

Then the hunter turned to ride back to camp. Waving his hat in farewell, he started off. George called out after him, "But you didn't tell us your name, stranger! What's your name?"

The hunter grinned. "William F. Cody," he called back. "Buffalo Bill, at your service!"

The two dudes were speechless. As the famous man disappeared over the hill, they realized that Jim had gotten his wish. But it was *he* who had learned a thing or two!

PECOS BILL, THE YOUTH
WHO TAMED THE WEST

Vocabulary Preview

coyote   [*ky O tee*]—small kind of wolf
The *coyote* was howling on the hill.
cyclone   [*SY klone*]—fierce wind storm
The *cyclone* tore up trees as it went rushing by.
invention   [*in VEN shun*]—something made or thought up for the first time
The electric light was Thomas Edison's *invention*.
lasso   [*LASS o*]—rope with a loop at the end for catching animals
The cowboy swung his *lasso* toward the wild bull.

Many people enjoy the rides at an amusement park. They love to fly high into the air on the Ferris wheel. They get a thrill from zooming up and down on rollercoasters that go so fast they take your breath away. Have you ever been on rides like that? Do you remember how you felt when you stepped off afterward?

Amusement park rides often have strange names—the Whip, the Tornado, the Caterpillar. So it should not surprise you to hear the names of the wild and dangerous things a cowboy named Pecos Bill went riding on.

Of course, Bill was not in an amusement park. And he didn't take his famous rides just for fun. As you read this story, you'll see that each ride taken by Pecos Bill was a part of his job of taming the Old West.

P<small>OOR LITTLE</small> B<small>ILL</small>! He was sitting in the Texas dust, watching his family's wagon go bouncing down the rocky road. He could see his nine brothers and ten sisters as they played inside the covered wagon. But not one of them noticed that their three-year-old brother had fallen out.

Little Bill didn't call to them. He thought maybe this was a new kind of game. He just watched the wagon disappear into the West. Then he waited to see what would happen next.

Soon the wagon was out of sight, and night began to fall. Coyotes came out to sit on the hilltops. Lifting their heads, they howled at the moon. Bill thought this must be part of the game too. So he started to howl. At first he didn't howl just right. But he kept on trying, until pretty soon he could howl as well as any coyote pup.

A grown-up coyote heard Bill. The animal ran down the hill to the lost child. "Now that's a mighty strange-looking coyote pup," the animal thought to himself. "But I'd better take it home with me anyway."

The coyote pups watched as Bill was led into their den. They howled with laughter.

"If that's a coyote, then I'm a rattlesnake," cried one pup.

"And he's got no tail," laughed another.

"His ears aren't even pointy," teased a third. He pulled one of Bill's ears to prove it.

Bill laughed. "What a wonderful game," he thought. He reached out and pulled the ears of the pups. But he didn't stop there. He swung the pups high into the air until they howled with pain. After that, they quickly learned to respect Bill. Not only did they let him stay, they even made him their leader. And that's how Bill got to be chief of the coyotes.

The years flew by. Bill grew very tall, and at thirteen years old he was still growing. His fame was growing too. All the animals in the West knew about Pecos Bill. They knew that he could beat up rattlesnakes, mountain lions and wild bears. Indeed, they knew that he could fight anything that flew, walked or crawled. Soon Bill came to be known as the West's king of beasts.

Now, this made a certain mountain lion very jealous. The lion felt that such a title belonged only to himself and to his cousins in Africa. "I can't let that coyote boy get away with this," thought the lion.

One morning, the lion saw Bill standing in front of a big rock. Bill was giving lessons to some coyote pups on how to howl. The lion climbed to the top of the rock and waited. Then, when Bill threw back his head to howl, the lion made a mighty leap. He knocked Bill into the dust. But the coyote chief didn't stay on the ground for long. Springing to his feet, he grabbed the lion around the middle.

"I could squeeze you to death," said Bill. "I've killed more than a hundred bears that way. But I have something else in store for you." Saying that, the boy leaped on the lion's back.

"Get off! Get off!" growled the mountain lion. He leaped and spat and shook himself wildly. But he couldn't get Bill off his back.

"I won't get off until you agree to do just as I say," called Bill.

"Never!" roared the lion. He began to leap and kick some more. He jumped from side to side and did flips in the air. But the boy just laughed and held on tight.

After a while the lion grew very tired. He stood there, panting for breath. "You win," he gasped finally. "Just spare my life, and I'll always carry you wherever you want to go."

Bill smiled, and the coyote pups cheered. But Bill held up his hand. "Sh," he said. "Listen. Do you hear what I hear?" Quickly he rode the lion to the top of a hill.

Looking down, Bill saw a two-legged creature running across the plain. It was a man, but Bill thought it was a coyote like himself. After all, he hadn't seen any fellow human beings since the day he fell out of the wagon.

The man had been moving a herd of cattle along a trail. But a longhorn bull had left the herd and was now chasing the cowboy. "Help! Help!" cried the poor man.

Bill didn't waste a second. He whistled loudly, and hundreds of rattlesnakes crawled out from under the nearby rocks. Slipping and sliding, they rushed toward Bill. He tied the snakes together, one after another, and made a loop at one end of his snake rope. It was the first lasso ever made, for these were the early days of the West, and things like lassos and hitching posts hadn't been invented yet. (In fact, Bill was later to become the greatest of all inventors.)

Bill could see that the cowboy had given up. The poor man had fallen to the ground. He was lying there with his face buried in his arms. The huge bull was rushing straight toward him.

Bill rode down the hill swinging his lasso in the air. Suddenly he sent it flying out over the bull. The loop came down over his huge horns. The surprised beast was pulled to a sudden stop. For a moment he looked around wildly. Then he started to struggle. He yanked and pulled to get free. How that beast kicked and tugged and snorted! He kept it up for a full half-hour. But he could have saved himself the trouble.

Bill gave a tug on the lasso that yanked the bull right off his feet. He swung the animal round and round in the air. When Bill let loose, the beast went flying over the plain for five miles.

Finally the scared cowboy opened his eyes and looked up. "I'm safe," he cried. "I'm safe!" Happily, he jumped to his feet. But then he froze in his tracks. He had caught sight of Pecos Bill and his friends.

"Mountain lion! Rattlesnakes!" cried the cowboy. And he began to shake from head to toe.

"Don't be frightened," called Bill. "They won't hurt you. They're my friends."

It took a while, but the cowboy finally saw that there was nothing to fear. In fact, Bill even taught him how to use the lasso.

"This is a great invention," said the cowboy. "It will help men to tame the West. I can't wait to tell my friends about this. And I'll tell them that you taught me to use it. Say, just who are you anyway?"

"A coyote," said Bill, "just like you. But to tell the truth, until now I thought that I was the only funny-looking coyote around these parts."

The cowboy laughed. "You're no coyote! You're a boy," he said. "You must have been lost out here for a long time. Why don't you come back to my ranch with me? You can teach all the cowboys how to use the lasso. And you can teach us how to tame animals so we can ride them."

Bill liked that idea. He went back to his coyote friends and told them he was going away for a while. "But I'll be back," he promised. Then Bill rode off on the back of his mountain lion.

Soon Bill was enjoying life as a cowboy teacher. He wore fancy cowboy clothes and cowboy boots. And he invented the ten-gallon hat to go with the rest of his outfit.

The cowboys liked him very much. They came from far and wide to take lessons from him. At first, he tried to teach them to ride mountain lions. But the men weren't too happy about the idea. That's when Bill thought of teaching them to bust bronchos. (That's cowboy talk that Bill made up. It just means that the men were taught to tame wild horses.)

Bill also taught the men to use lassos. The cowboys made theirs out of rope, but Bill stuck to his famous snake lasso. He did many wonderful tricks with it, and people from all over the country came to see him perform.

The most famous use of Bill's lasso took place one day in March. That morning, a band of cowboys came riding up to Bill. "Run for your life!" they shouted. "A big cyclone is on its way. And they say that it's coming to get *you*!"

During the weeks before this, the cyclone had been very

busy tearing up towns in Oklahoma and Arizona. But when it heard about Pecos Bill and his famous lasso, the cyclone came tearing into Texas.

Everyone but Bill ran to hide. He'd never seen a cyclone before, so he just waited in the front yard for it to come along. While he waited, he invented a few things. In the first five minutes, he invented cow-punching and the hitching post. In the next five minutes, he thought up the sheriff's star, law and order and the Pony Express. He would have invented a few more things too, but just then the cyclone came spinning into view.

Bill stared calmly at the great twister. "So you're after me, are you?" he said to himself. "We'll soon see about that." Then Bill gave a loud whistle, and every rattler in Texas rushed up to him. Within minutes, Bill had a lasso that could reach to New Mexico and back.

The cyclone came tearing along. To show its strength, it sent houses and horses flying into the air. And all the while, it kept its eye on Bill.

Bill waited until the cyclone was just a mile away. Then —*whoosh! whoosh!*—the lasso went spinning into the sky. It cut through the clouds and dropped right over the top of the cyclone.

This made the cyclone so angry that it leaped ten miles into the sky. Bill just held onto his lasso. Then, hand over hand, he started to pull himself up. Finally he was sitting on the cyclone's back.

The cyclone flew into a rage. It flipped forward and backward and sideways. It shook like five thousand wild horses.

"Ho-hum," said Bill. "I wish I had something exciting to do today."

When the cyclone heard that, it grew wilder than ever. It

206

bounced like ten thousand wild bulls. It crashed through canyons and leaped over mountains. It shivered and shook. It twisted and turned. But it couldn't shake Bill off its back. The wild ride went on until the cyclone was almost out of wind. Then it began to get smaller and smaller. Soon it was only a breeze.

Some people say the cyclone rained itself out under Pecos Bill. But Bill told his friends that the cyclone had really cried itself out. He said he had even heard the poor worn-out thing sobbing.

Only after the cyclone had promised to be nice to people from then on did Bill let it go. And the cyclone has kept its promise. In fact, you may have met the worn-out cyclone yourself and not known it. It's that sudden little breeze that makes people feel so good on hot summer evenings.

THE STRANGE ARMIES
FROM THE SKY

locust   [*LO kust*]—kind of insect
       The *locust* looks like a grasshopper.
swarm   [*SWORM*]—big crowd
       A *swarm* of bees flew toward the beehive.

When we hear the word *farmer,* do we usually think of the word *hero* at the same time? Probably not. But the hard-working farmer really is something of a hero.

He faces long, hard hours under the hot sun. Sometimes he has to fight the dangers of flood, fire and terrible storms. And yet, through thick and thin, he gets his crops grown so that we can buy them for our dinner tables.

The story that follows is about a brave farm family. When faced with a strange enemy, they didn't run away. Instead, they stood their ground and fought to save their land and crops.

Read to find out how they faced the danger from the sky.

No ONE would have thought such a strange thing could happen in the valley of Salt Lake, Utah, in the late 1800's. It was a day like any other. The farmers were busy tending their crops. And the women were busy with their housework.

Just before noon, three teen-age brothers had finished their work and were playing a game of hide-and-seek. Joseph closed his eyes to count to fifty. Frank and William ran to find hiding places. William climbed up into a tree. Frank looked around and then jumped into a barrel.

When Joseph had closed his eyes, the sun was shining. But when he opened his eyes, the sun was gone! The sky was almost dark.

"William," he called. "Something's wrong up in the sky."

William stuck his head out through the leaves and stared at the sky. "It's a big cloud over the sun," he said. "It's the biggest storm cloud I've ever seen!"

Frank hopped out of the barrel. "Come on," he called.

"We've got to tell Father about this!" They ran toward the barn.

Moments later, the boys came dashing back into the yard with their father. There was fear in his eyes.

Looking up at the sky, he shook his head. "That's not a storm cloud," he said. "It's an army of locusts! Those insects can eat up every grain of wheat or corn in a minute flat. We've got to stop them!"

Father and the boys raced toward the house. As they ran, they looked back again and again. They could see the locusts sweeping down on the fields.

Father had a plan. He told his family to gather up all the blankets in the house. Then he grabbed a broom and ran out to get his big farm shovel. Soon the whole family was running toward the fields.

All at once the locusts seemed to be everywhere! They covered the fields! The wings of the insects buzzed as loud as thunder as they rushed to attack the crops. They paid no attention to the frightened family.

Quickly, Father shook open a blanket. He threw it over a whole swarm of insects. Then he began to beat the blanket with his shovel. Mother and the boys threw their blankets over more locusts. Mother beat down on her blanket with the broom.

"Jump!" Father cried to his sons. "Jump on your blankets!" The boys did as they were told. They jumped up and down as hard as they could.

The family ran from field to field. They kept on throwing blankets over the swarms of insects and then beating the locusts that were trapped. The fight went on and on. As the family worked, they prayed that the locusts would not kill every growing thing.

Now the whole sky was dark with the pests. There seemed to be no end to their number. More and more of them came buzzing down. Soon all the farms for miles around were covered with them.

"Don't give up!" Father shouted. "Don't give up! Maybe we can save just a few of the crops!"

The family didn't stop to breathe. They just kept hitting at the locusts.

A short while later, Mother looked up at the sky. Now she saw something different! "A big gray cloud is moving this way," she cried. "What is it? Can it be rain? What's going to happen now?"

Father and the boys didn't know what to think. They looked quickly at the gray cloud. But they were too busy fighting for their crops to talk.

The gray cloud grew brighter and brighter as it swept toward the fields. Soon the family could see that this was not a cloud at all. It was a second army in the sky!

"Sea gulls!" Joseph cried. "It's a whole army of sea gulls! Look at those birds! There are thousands of them!"

The family couldn't believe their eyes. "Sea gulls?" Father exclaimed. "Why, no sea gull has ever been seen *here* before!"

It was true that sea gulls had never been seen so far from water. But they were a welcome sight to the farmers. The army of birds swooped down onto the fields. With loud cries and beating wings, the birds attacked the locusts.

Wave after wave of birds swooped down. As each group of gulls reached the ground, they gobbled up hundreds of locusts. Soon the buzzing sound of the insects grew softer. Then, at last, there was silence. The birds had eaten up every locust in sight.

Then, almost as if it had received a signal from a leader, the sea gull army rose into the air. The birds flew off together toward the Great Salt Lake.

The farmer was too tired to say anything. He could only stare at the birds until they were out of sight. Then he looked at his fields. Enough of the crops were left to feed his family through the coming winter.

Now the sun was shining once again. Everything seemed peaceful, as if nothing special had happened that day. But all the people in the valley knew it was a day that would never be forgotten.

THE GIANT WHO COULD
SOLVE ANY PROBLEM

dismal   [*DIZ mul*]—gloomy; not cheerful
The dark, empty room was very *dismal.*
mosquito   [*mo SKEE toe*]—kind of flying insect that bites
The crying baby had been stung by a *mosquito.*
pluck   [*PLUK*]—pick
John went to *pluck* flowers from the garden.
progress   [*PRAHG res*]—move forward; improvement
Jim made *progress* in all his school work.
syrup   [*SIR up*]—sweet, sticky liquid
The children liked *syrup* on their pancakes.

Have you ever wished you could get your hands on Aladdin's magic lamp? Just imagine having a lamp with a genie in it who could solve all your problems! According to ancient belief, a genie was a spirit who appeared as a giant, and who could get all kinds of impossible things done.

Such a genie could help you with your homework or carry you to faraway places (after school, of course). What a friend to have!

This story is about Febold Feboldson. He was not a genie, but he might just as well have been. He was such a giant of a man that he could solve any problem that came his way. He even solved the problem of the giant mosquitoes!

ONE MORNING long ago, a little girl in New York City went to her front window to put crumbs on the sill. Then she waited for the birds to come eat them.

She didn't see any birds, but what she did see made her rub her eyes to be sure she was awake.

"A giant!" she cried. "There's a giant outside!"

"This is no time for jokes," said the girl's mother. "I'm very busy."

"*Please* come here!" begged the child. "Tell me if I'm seeing things!"

The little girl wasn't joking. So her mother ran to the window. Sure enough, *there was a giant of a man outside!* He had a suitcase under his left arm. And under his right arm he carefully held a sleeping man.

On the sidewalk, people were staring and stepping out of the giant's way. But they didn't seem frightened. The blond giant was smiling and waving to them.

"Who are you?" called one man. "Where are you from?"

"My name is Febold Feboldson," said the giant. "And my sleeping friend is Mr. Johnson. We've just come from Sweden."

"What a wonderful fellow! Stay here with us," cried the man. "We'll make you our mayor."

"That's very nice of you," said Febold. "But it's too crowded here for me. There's no room for me to stretch my legs. I'm heading for the West. I want to see open lands."

There were no trains or horses big enough to carry Febold. He had to walk. But he didn't mind. The miles were no problem to him. Febold was a giant who took giant steps.

It took just three hundred steps for Febold to reach Nebraska. When he got there, something about this land made him stop to have a long look at it. He had a feeling that it might be a good place to live.

About that time, Mr. Johnson woke up. "Look at that dismal river," he said. "The land looks dismal too. But somehow I like it. Let's stop here for a bit."

Febold put Mr. Johnson down. "We'll do better than that," said Febold. "We'll settle here!"

Mr. Johnson looked around once more. "But the land is so flat. And there are no trees," he said. "However, I suppose you can take care of that, Febold. You can solve any problem. We'll start working on it just as soon as I wake up." Then Mr. Johnson curled up on the ground and was soon fast asleep again.

Febold didn't waste time, however. He rushed around to nearby states and plucked up a few forests. He planted these in Nebraska and then got busy with some other work. He worked all through the night.

When Mr. Johnson woke up the next morning, he thought

he was back home in Sweden. He found himself in a house! Febold had built it around him while he slept.

Mr. Johnson rushed outside. His eyes sparkled with joy. There were valleys and hills all around! And there were cottonwood trees on the hills! Groves of willow trees lined the river banks!

He looked up at the giant, who was leaning on a great shovel. "How fresh! How green it all is!" cried Mr. Johnson. "Febold, you've solved the problem of the treeless plain!"

Mr. Johnson rushed back into the house. He sat down at once to write to his family in Sweden. Soon many of them came over to America. (That's why there are so many Johnsons in Nebraska now.)

While Mr. Johnson was in the house, Febold opened his big bag. He took out some seeds, a horse and a plow. Then he went off to plant crops.

Febold didn't know it, but he would soon have more problems to solve. One was the great killer mosquitoes. Another was what to do with the giant popcorn balls. But he didn't have to worry about them just yet.

Febold got to work. He planted row after row of corn in the fields. Then he climbed the high hills and planted sugar cane. He worked long and hard. He didn't stop until the moon came out. Then Febold wiped his brow. "Time to go home," he said.

When he turned to leave, he saw that some of his crops were already half grown. "Such fine land," he exclaimed. "I'm glad this is my home now."

But then, as he stood there, he heard a great buzzing noise. Looking up, Febold saw hundreds of mosquitoes. They were huge! And they looked wild and mean.

One of them flew down toward Febold. The insect was as

big as three cows, but Febold wasn't afraid. He stood his ground.

Pointing to the land, the insect buzzed loud and long. With his wings, the insect beat his chest.

"Are you telling me you want this land?" asked Febold. The insect buzzed again.

"But this is my land!" cried Febold. "I've worked for it. You can't just come here and take it!"

The chief insect's eyes flashed red. He waved the sharp tip of his long stinger. Febold knew that this was a warning.

"No!" cried Febold. He pulled himself up straight and tall. "You can't have my crops or my land!"

The mosquito chief shook with rage. He shot up into the air to talk to the other insects. Soon their buzzing grew as loud as thunder! Then, all together, they flew toward Febold.

How could the giant save himself from these killers? What could he do? Quickly he turned and ran into the house. His giant steps took him there in five seconds. Inside, he pulled a hammer and an iron pot out of his bag. Then he ran for the open fields.

The pot Febold carried was a soup kettle. It was huge. It had to be, for Febold cooked his giant meals in it.

Zzzzzzzz! The mosquitoes rushed after him. Their eyes blazed like fire!

Suddenly Febold stopped running. He turned the pot upside down and slipped under it. Would he be safe from the killer insects?

The insect chief picked up speed. He planned to crash right into the pot and turn it over. With his head down, he zoomed forward. *Bang!* His head hit the pot like a huge bullet. But the pot didn't move an inch.

A great bump appeared on the chief's head. The other

insects buzzed with laughter as he rubbed it. Now he was angry, so he flew up to try again. With a buzz and a flip, the great mosquito zoomed down once more.

Down, down, down he sped. This time his great stinger was aimed at the pot!

Zing! The sharp stinger tore right through the pot. The other insects cheered. But they stopped when their chief began buzzing for help. He couldn't get his stinger out of the pot! The insects tugged and tugged. But they couldn't pull their leader free. He was stuck fast.

Now they were all wild with anger! They shot up into the air. Then they zoomed down from all sides. Their stingers flashed like steel swords.

Zing! Zing! Zing! The mosquitoes' stingers ripped through the iron pot. They had easily pierced the big kettle. But getting free again was a different story! Not one insect could pull his stinger loose. Febold was seeing to that!

As each stinger came through the pot, Febold hit it as hard as he could with his hammer. Once it was bent, the insect couldn't pull his stinger out of the kettle.

Zing! Zing! Zing! More stingers cut through the pot. Soon all the mosquitoes were trapped with their stingers inside the pot. How they buzzed and tugged and shook themselves! But it didn't do any good.

When they were all caught, Febold lifted the pot and jumped out. Picking up his gun, he made short work of the fearful killers. "Now," he said, "I guess they won't be stealing anyone's crops or land!"

Febold looked up. It was morning! "Time to tend my crops," he said to himself. So he walked back to the fields he had planted.

Febold wasn't surprised to see the crops full grown. (After

all, he was in Nebraska!) But he was surprised to see the strange weather over his farm. The weather was in stripes! That's right—stripes!

There was a mile-wide stripe of sunshine, a mile-wide stripe of rain, another stripe of sunshine and so on. The sugar cane was under stripes of rain. The corn was baking under stripes of sunshine.

Soon the corn became so hot that it started to pop. Popcorn shot through the air. *Pop! Pop! Pop!* In a few minutes, popcorn covered the ground. It looked like a blanket of snow.

Febold looked up at the sugar cane on the hills. The rain was washing the syrup right out of the cane. Soon there were puddles of syrup everywhere. Then the puddles ran down the hills in streams. And where were the streams heading? Right toward the fields of corn!

The syrup splashed into the corn. The heaps of corn began to roll along the fields. The corn and syrup mixed together into giant popcorn balls. On and on they went spinning, like great snowballs.

That night, when the sun went down, there were hundreds and hundreds of popcorn balls in the fields. Some of them were hundreds of feet high. They looked like mountains of snow.

Febold stared at the popcorn balls. But was he cross about having his first crops turn out this way? Of course not. Febold was all for progress. "I'm glad the popcorn ball has been invented at last," he said. "I'll send them all over the land for people to enjoy!"

Yes, there wasn't a problem Febold couldn't solve. And to this day, folks in Nebraska talk about the giant from Sweden. "Why, if Febold Feboldson were here now," they say, "we'd have no problems at all!"

THE CELEBRATED
JUMPING FROG

celebrated [*SELL e bray ted*]—famous, talked about
Crowds turned out to see the *celebrated* actor.

county [*KOWN tee*]—part of a state
Each *county* in the state had its own spelling-bee champion.

disgusted [*diss GUST ed*]—sickened, let down
The scientist was *disgusted* with the results of his experiment.

sly [*SLY*]—acting in a secret way; tricky
Few people trust a *sly* man.

weighs [*WAZE*]—measures how heavy a person or thing is
He *weighs* the bag of fruit.

wobble [*WAHB l*]—shake
The boy's legs began to *wobble* when he saw the bear.

Young athletes often practice different kinds of jumping—the broad jump and high jump, for example. Can you think of any games in which the ability to jump plays an important part?

Not long ago, a schoolboy leaped to a height of over six feet in a city-wide contest. In so doing, he almost broke what was then the world's high-jump record.

If Jim Smiley had been there to see the contest, he would have tried to make a bet on how things would turn out. Jim thought he knew a lot about jumping contests. And he was one of those people who would bet on anything.

This tale, based on Mark Twain's funny story, tells you about some of Jim Smiley's amazing bets. (And if Jim were here now, he'd bet you couldn't read it in ten minutes.)

FOLKS IN Calaveras, California, never said good morning to Jim Smiley. They were afraid he would try to bet them that it *wasn't* a good morning. Yes sir, Jim would bet on anything!

If there was a horse race, Jim would bet on it. If there was a chicken fight, Jim would bet on that too. And he didn't care which side he bet on, as long as he had a bet.

One day, Jim and another fellow were out walking. They saw two birds sitting on a fence. "Say," spoke up Jim. "Let's bet on those two birds."

"Bet on those birds?" said his friend. "What's there to bet on? Those birds are just sitting there."

Jim scratched the back of his neck. "Well," he said at last, "let's bet on which one will fly away first!"

The next day, Jim saw the town preacher, Parson Walker. The Parson's wife had been awfully sick. In fact, it looked as if she might never get well.

Jim nodded to the Parson. "How's your wife today?" he asked.

Parson Walker's eyes lit up. "She sat up in bed this morning," he said. "And she was smiling. All at once she seems to be getting better. With the Lord's help, she'll get well yet!"

"Hm," said Jim, digging into his pocket. "I'll bet two and a half dollars that she *won't!*"

Yes sir, Jim Smiley would bet on *anything.*

That afternoon, Jim went home to get his horse. This horse was the most broken-down nag you ever did see. She looked as if she had every disease ever invented. She coughed and wheezed, and she walked as if all four feet hurt. But, for all that, she had won Jim many a bet.

Jim led his horse down the street. Seeing a stranger, Jim stopped. He patted his horse on the nose. "Easy, Star," he said. "A racer like you must save her strength." Jim grinned to himself. He knew the stranger was listening.

The stranger looked at Star. "You call that thing a *racer?*" he sneered.

"Not *just* a racer," answered Jim. "This is the fastest horse in Calaveras County! She can beat any horse of yours, and I'll bet on it!"

The stranger took another look at Star, snorting and wobbling on her thin legs.

"You're sure you want to bet?" he asked.

"I'm sure," said Jim. "You just get your horse. I'll race you to that big oak tree down the road. The tree will be our finish line."

Star rolled her sad eyes at Jim and coughed a weak little cough.

The stranger laughed out loud. "I'll take your bet," he said. "What's more, I'll give your *racer* a hundred-yard head start." Still laughing, he went off to get his horse. Soon he was back on a beautiful young animal. The horse had bright eyes, strong legs and a shiny brown coat.

By now, a group of men had gathered to see the fun. They helped Jim climb up on old Star's back. Poor Star! Her back almost caved in when Jim sat in the saddle. She coughed again, a loud, sad cough.

Jim rode Star a hundred yards down the road. Then the stranger gave his horse a slap, and the race was on. The brown horse leaped forward and sped down the road. In a few seconds he was halfway up to Star. In a few more seconds, he had passed her.

The stranger looked back. "Come on, catch up!" he laughed. But Star only began to cough again. Her poor old body shook from head to tail. The stranger roared with laughter. Even his horse seemed to be grinning.

Still, Jim didn't look worried. He was waiting for something to happen. And happen it did! Suddenly Star, all warmed up at last, leaped forward. Jim held on tight!

Now Star flashed up the road. Her legs were like flapping wings, kicking this way and that. She coughed and sneezed and puffed through her nose. And what a racket she made as she kicked up the dust!

When the stranger looked back again, he couldn't believe his eyes. "It can't be!" he shouted. "That beast was almost dead!"

The stranger whipped his horse. "Faster, faster!" he yelled. "We're almost to the finish line!"

It was true. The finish line was just twelve yards away. Soon the stranger's horse was only inches from it. But Star's nose was already over the line!

The stranger shook his head. "Your horse sure fooled me,"

he said. "Here's your money. You won it fair and square." He paid Jim and rode off, still shaking his head.

Jim rode home with the money jingling in his pocket. But soon he was back in town again. This time he was carrying a little wooden box. In the box was his wonderful jumping frog, Daniel Webster.

Jim had been training Daniel all year, until that frog was the best jumper around. Why, Daniel Webster could jump clear over a tall horse's back. No other frog in the state could do that!

Now Jim headed for the hotel. If he was lucky, he would meet another stranger there. He didn't have to wait long. A strange man was standing by the hotel door. He looked at Jim.

"What's in that box?" asked the man.

Jim smiled slyly. "It could be a parrot, but it isn't," he said. "And it could be a canary, but it isn't."

Jim opened the box. "It's a frog."

The stranger stared at Daniel Webster. "Hm," he said, "so it is. Well, what's he good for?"

"Well," said Jim, "he's good for *one* thing. He can outjump any other frog in Calaveras County."

The stranger folded his arms. He rocked back and forth on his heels. "I don't see anything about that frog that's so different from any other," he said.

"Maybe you don't," said Jim. "Maybe you understand frogs and maybe you don't. Maybe you've had experience and maybe you haven't. But *I* have. And I'll bet forty dollars that this frog can outjump any other in Calaveras County."

The stranger thought a minute. Then he said, "Well, I'm only a stranger here, and I don't have a frog. But if I *had* a frog, I'd bet you."

228

"That's all right!" said Jim. "If you'll hold my box a minute, I'll go and get you a frog." So the stranger took the box, put up his forty dollars and sat down to wait.

He sat there a long time, thinking and thinking. Finally he took Jim's frog out of the box. Then he took out a bag of gunshot. He forced the frog's mouth open and poured the shot into it. When the frog was filled up nearly to his chin, the stranger set him on the floor.

Meanwhile, Jim Smiley was at the swamp, stomping around in the mud looking for a frog. Finally he caught one and brought it back to the stranger.

"Now," said Jim, "if you're ready, let's start."

The stranger put his frog on the floor next to Daniel Webster. Then Jim counted, "One—two—three!" At the count of three, each man gave his frog a push. The stranger's frog hopped off smartly. But Daniel Webster just hunched his shoulders and sat there. He couldn't move an inch.

Jim was pretty surprised, and he was disgusted too. "I can't figure it out," he said. "Why, I trained that frog myself!"

Jim had no choice. He took out forty dollars and handed it to the stranger. The man took the money and started away. But as he was going out the door, he turned. "Well," he said, "I still don't see anything about that frog that's different from any other."

Poor Jim stood scratching his head and looking at Daniel for a long time. Finally he picked up his frog. "What's this?" he cried. "This frog weighs more than five pounds!" Then he turned Daniel Webster upside down, and the gunshot came spilling out. When he saw what was what, Jim Smiley was the maddest man in Calaveras County.

"I've been tricked!" he yelled. "I've been robbed! That's what comes of betting. I'll never make a bet again!" With that, he ran out of the hotel and dashed down the road after the stranger.

As he ran, he passed one of his friends.

"Where you going, Jim?" called his friend.

"To catch a thief!" yelped Jim. "He's got a head start, but I'll catch him all right. I'll bet you five dollars!"

A TALE OF
FLYING SAUCERS

description [*de SKRIP shun*]—report of how a person or thing looks or acts
The police asked for a *description* of the stolen car.

hovering [*HUV er ing*]—staying in one place in the air
The bird was *hovering* over its nest.

object [*OB jekt*]—thing that a person can see or touch
The heavy *object* crashed to the ground.

scientist [*SY in tist*]—person skilled in science
George Washington Carver was a *scientist* who made 300 different products from the peanut.

soiled [*SOYLD*]—made dirty; not clean
The children *soiled* their clothes with glue and paint.

unidentified [*un i DEN ti fide*]—not known or called by name
The man in the picture was *unidentified.*

From its title, do you think that the story you are about to read is a true one? It is no more false or true than many of the legends you have read in this book.

There is something else you should know. The descriptions of the flying saucers are based on those given to newspapers by people who claim to have really seen them. *Everything told about the saucers in this story is true, according to someone.*

Will this tale prove whether or not there are such things as flying saucers? That is something you will have to decide for yourself, after you have read the story.

Two CALIFORNIA teen-agers, Ted and Don, were on their way home from basketball practice at the community center. It was just about nine o'clock.

"I wish Coach Watson had been there to see us tonight," said Don. "We played pretty well, didn't we?"

"Sure, but it was only practice tonight," Ted answered. "Let's hope we play like that at the next school game. I don't like to remember last week's game."

Don nodded. "Yes, we really looked bad. And with all those girls from our class watching us too!" he added. "Do you remember the look on the coach's face when I missed that last shot?"

Don laughed and waited for Ted to answer him. But when there was no answer, Don turned around to look at his teammate. His friend wasn't with him. Ted had stopped walking about ten feet back. His eyes were fixed on the sky.

"What's wrong?" called Don. He looked up to see what Ted was staring at.

A noiseless object was hovering about two hundred feet above their heads. It was shaped like a huge saucer. Sometimes it seemed to glow a little, and there was a band of blue light around its edges.

"Can this really be happening?" Don whispered. All at once he remembered the newspaper stories he had read several months before. Maybe those people in South America hadn't been seeing things! One man claimed he had even taken a picture of one of the strange objects!

The two boys stood where they were without moving a muscle. They watched as a small dot of red light appeared in the middle of the object. The light became a beam, growing wider as it reached the ground. Like a great searchlight, it swept over the countryside.

Then a film of gray stuff, soft as smoke, floated down from the saucer. It fell over the trees, the telephone poles and the two frightened boys.

Suddenly the beam and the gray, lacey stuff began to rush back toward the object. Soon the light was just a bright red speck again.

As the boys watched, six more objects sped silently through the sky. The one just over the boys shot up and joined the group. In a matter of seconds, the line of seven objects was out of sight.

A few minutes went by before the boys could find strength to move and speak. "What—what were those things? And that strange light?" mumbled Ted at last.

Don didn't answer. He just picked up the bag he had dropped and started to walk. Ted caught up with him. Then the boys broke into a run. They ran faster than they had ever run on any basketball court.

When they were almost out of breath, they slowed to a

234

walk again. But it was a fast walk! As they hurried along, Ted asked, "Do you think those things were the flying saucers people were talking about a few months ago?"

"I don't know," answered Don. "I'm just wondering what we should do now."

"Call the police, I guess," answered Ted. He was silent for a moment. Then he added, "Do you think they'll believe us?"

Don didn't answer. He was remembering how his neighbors used to tap their foreheads and make jokes about people who claimed to have seen flying saucers.

As the boys reached their block, they slowed down. The houses and lights they knew so well made them feel a little better.

"I don't think we should call the police about this until we talk to a scientist," said Don. "Maybe there's a good explanation for what we saw."

Ted nodded. "You're right. It might save us from making fools of ourselves. But don't you think we should at least tell our parents when we get home?"

"Maybe," answered Don. "Let's wait and see."

The boys hurried up the front steps of their apartment house. They went into Don's first-floor apartment. Don's father looked up from his newspaper. "How was practice?" he asked. "Any better than——?"

Just at that moment, a news flash came over the radio: "Mr. and Mrs. Joris of East Elm Street claim that they saw a strange object in the sky tonight. It was flashing a red light across the ground for several blocks. The police are looking into the matter now."

Click! Don's mother turned off the radio. "That's a wild story," she said. "Why do people make up such tales? Do they just want to see their names in the paper?"

"But what if they're telling the truth?" asked Don.

"If I thought those tales were true, I'd have trouble sleeping at night," she answered. There was a look of real fear in her eyes.

Don's father and the boys saw this. His father changed the subject. Turning to Don, he asked, "How was practice tonight? Any better than the little show at school last week?" He grinned a little.

"Uh—well, it was all right," answered his son. "I guess I'll say good night now. I've got to get up early in the morning. There's something I want to talk over with Doctor Storm before I go to school."

"Doctor Storm, the new scientist at the big plant on Rowe Street?" asked the father.

"Yes," said Don. "Doctor Storm spoke to our science class a few days ago. He said we were welcome to drop in and ask him questions any morning before nine o'clock."

Ted agreed to meet Don at eight o'clock the next morning. Then he climbed the stairs to his family's apartment. He had also decided not to tell his family about the strange objects.

Neither of the two boys could sleep very well that night. Don tried to read a magazine, but he couldn't keep his mind on the words. He decided to get things ready for the next day. He got up and went to put some fresh socks into his equipment bag.

Reaching for the canvas bag, he saw that he had forgotten to close it. When he looked into it, his eyes flew open. Some of the gray stuff had stuck to one of his soiled socks. Now the stuff had grown thicker. It looked like a web.

Don quickly rolled the sock in a magazine and hid it in his bag. Then he climbed back into bed. He couldn't wait for morning to come. He *had* to speak to Doctor Storm.

236

The next morning Don gulped down his breakfast. Then he picked up his books and equipment bag. "So long!" he called to his parents as he dashed out the door.

Ted was waiting outside. The boys didn't waste any time. As they ran toward the plant, Don told his friend about the gray, weblike stuff hidden in his equipment bag.

Soon the boys reached the plant. A friendly guard walked with them to Doctor Storm's laboratory. "Hello, boys!" said the scientist. He was just putting on his long white coat. He asked the boys their names. Then he said, "I'm glad to see that you were interested enough in my talk to come and see me. Is there something you want me to go over again?"

"Well," said Ted. "It's not about the talk you gave at school. . . ."

"What is it then?" asked Doctor Storm.

"It's about these flying-saucer stories," said Don.

Doctor Storm laughed. "I'm afraid that's all they are," he said. "Just stories!"

Don shook his head. "No, Doctor Storm," said the boy. "We saw them ourselves. And I can prove it."

The scientist's gray eyes flashed. "How?" he snapped. "How can you prove it?"

Don was beginning to feel afraid of the scientist. But he started to tell him about the morning's discovery.

"I don't believe it," said Doctor Storm. "You'll have to show me the web first."

Don thought to himself for a moment. "I—I left it at home," he finally said. "It's in my closet."

Ted's eyes opened wide when he heard that. But Don's look made him keep still.

Don went on, "I'll bring it to you after school."

"Yes, yes," said Doctor Storm. "You do that. But now you'll have to excuse me. I have lots of work to do."

As the boys left the plant, Ted asked in a puzzled voice, "Why didn't you give the stuff to Doctor Storm?"

"Maybe I'm crazy," Don said. "Something told me not to. A hunch, I guess."

The boys had to run to get to school on time. They had a great deal of trouble with school that day. They couldn't keep their minds on their work at all. And during basketball practice, they kept dropping the ball and bumping into the other boys. The coach finally had to ask them to leave the court.

As they hurried home that afternoon, Don bought a newspaper. He wanted to see if the police had found out anything more about what that man and his wife had seen. All at once Don's eyes opened wide. He saw a headline that read, *"UFO Seen in New Jersey."*

"UFO?" said Ted. "Doesn't that mean *unidentified flying object?*"

"Right," answered Don. "And this story says that a girl in New Jersey claims to have seen *more* than one. It says that she saw them around twelve at night. *And her description of them matches our own!*"

"But—wait a minute!" cried Ted. "She saw them at midnight in New Jersey. But with the time difference of three hours, that means that she saw them at the same time we did! How can they have been in different places at the same time?"

The two friends stared at each other.

"Maybe there are lots of them," answered Don. "Or maybe. . . ."

"Maybe what?" asked Ted. "Maybe what?"

Don thought hard for a moment. "Yes, yes," he said finally. "Do you remember how fast those things flew away? Maybe they *did* cross the whole country in just a few minutes!"

By this time the boys had reached their block. They could see a crowd of people standing in front of their apartment house. The boys ran up to the building just as a policeman came out.

"What's wrong?" called Don. "We live here. Tell us what's happened!"

The policeman wouldn't let the boys enter the building. "Easy, boys," he said. "There's just been a little trouble in apartment 1C."

Don's mouth dropped open. That was his apartment!

The policeman went on, "Nobody's been hurt. We caught a burglar in there. Some neighbors called and said they had seen a man climbing into a back window. We got here just in time." At that moment, the front door swung open. "Here he is now!" said the policeman.

Ted and Don could hardly believe their eyes. They saw Doctor Storm being led out by two policemen. And there was an Air Force officer with them.

The boys pushed through the crowd and ran into Don's apartment. They were met by a man in an Air Force uniform.

"Who are you?" asked Don. "What are you doing in our apartment?"

"The Air Force has been following the man who was just taken out of here," said the officer.

"But what do you want with Doctor Storm?" asked Don.

The officer shook his head. "That's not his name. But it doesn't matter. We've got him now. All I can say is that you've done a great service to your country in helping us catch him. By the way, what was he looking for in your closet?"

Don gave the officer his equipment bag. Then he told him what had happened in Doctor Storm's office that morning.

"Why did you change your mind?" the officer asked.

"I felt that Doctor Storm knew more than he was telling. He asked me to show him the *web*. I had never called it that. How did he know what it was? That's when I made up my mind to tell my parents and the police everything as soon as I could."

"That was fast thinking," said the officer. "We'll put the gray stuff through every test we have. Then we'll know what steps to take next."

The officer thanked the boys again and left. Don sat down on the edge of his bed. He couldn't help thinking about Doctor Storm. Why had he broken into the apartment? Was he just a scientist who wanted to be the first to study the strange gray stuff? Was he an agent for another country? Or was he working, perhaps, for creatures from another planet?

Ted's voice interrupted Don's thinking. "We'll have to tell our parents now," he said. "They have a right to know."

Don nodded. "Yes, our parents will believe us," he said. "But will anyone else?"

Standing at the window, Ted looked up at the sunny sky. It was so blue and peaceful. "I doubt it," he said. "I doubt it very much."

In the weeks that followed, the boys watched the newspapers for a story about Doctor Storm. But there was no mention of him at all. In fact, they never heard of him again after that day he was taken away.

And when Don and Ted wrote to the Air Force for information about the doctor and the flying saucers, the boys were told that there was no information that could be given to them at that time. . . .

In the weeks that followed, the boys went to the community center for practice many times. But they always took a different route from the one they had taken the night the strange objects appeared in the sky. Indeed, the weeks turned into months before the boys found the courage to walk through that part of town again.

THE SEARCH FOR
THE RANCHERO'S
LOST TREASURE

Vocabulary Preview

brilliant   [*BRIL yent*]—sparkling, shining
A diamond is a *brilliant* stone.

dazzling   [*DAZ ling*]—of almost blinding brightness
The sunshine striking the clear water made a *dazzling* light.

fiesta   [*fee ES tuh*]—feast, special day, or celebration
There was dancing, singing, and good food at the *fiesta*.

mezcla   [*MEZ kluh*]—Spanish word for mud cement
The farmer stored some tools in the *mezcla* hut.

pastor   [*pas TOR*]—Spanish word for shepherd
The brave *pastor* chased a wolf away from the sheep.

ranchero   [*ran CHAIR o*]—Spanish word for a ranch owner
The *ranchero* paid his workers once a month.

244

Have you ever dreamed of finding lost treasure? If you have, you share a dream with almost every other human being. Tales about lost riches have excited men's imagination throughout the ages.

Western folklore is filled with stories of lost gold mines and hidden treasures. To this very day, people thrill to tales about the lost golden cities of Cibola. Coronado, the Spanish explorer was looking for those cities when he explored the Southwest.

Folks still sit wide-eyed, as they trade tales about mines like the Lost Dutchman mine, in Arizona. Can you think of any other famous lost mines or hidden treasures?

Here is a new version of a J. Frank Dobie story about another hidden treasure of the west. Was the ranchero's treasure ever found, or is it still "lost"? Read on to discover the answer for yourself.

MANY YEARS AGO, much of the land along the Nueces River in Texas belonged to rancheros. Rancheros were the owners of big ranches. Some of them became very rich, selling wool and sheep. Since there were no banks in those days, the rancheros hid their gold and silver in secret places in their homes and on their land.

Now, there was one ranchero who was more fortunate than the others, because he had the best workers in the whole territory. In fact, one of his men was praised far and wide. He was a pastor, or shepherd, known as "the pastor who never gives up." If even a single sheep was missing from one of the flocks, Pedro, the pastor, would search and search, even on his own free time, until he found the lost animal.

With helpers like Pedro, the ranchero soon became the richest ranchero of all. In time, word got around that he had a great treasure hidden away. The stories about his riches began to excite many robbers and bandits.

"There are bags of gold in his walls, and his furniture is silver painted over to look like wood," a bandit chief told his men as they sat around their campfire. The bandits listened, with greed burning in their eyes. They were eager to go after the treasure, but they had to be careful. They waited in their camp until the day word reached them that all the ranch workers had gone off to a wedding fiesta.

That night the bandits rode to the ranch house. They were sure they knew all the hiding places for the treasure. They lost no time in killing the ranchero so they could search. They looked under the bed and cut open the mattress, but they found neither gold nor silver. They tore holes in the walls. They dug up the dirt floor. In all these places they found nothing. Finally they chopped up the furniture and found that it was made of wood, just plain wood.

"Why, the old rascal has tricked us," growled the bandit chief. "The treasure must be buried outside."

Now the bandits began riding around the ranch, looking for clues. After a while, they came to the top of a high hill and searched around. They were just giving up when they spotted some dry twigs. The twigs were broken off where someone had gone into the thick bushes. The robbers quickly began cutting a path through the thick tangles of bushes and trees.

Suddenly the night was filled with terrible screams. "Aiee! Help!" howled a bandit. "The ranchero's ghost is reaching out to carry us away!" Then, all the bandits, except the chief, fell to the ground, trembling and crying for mercy.

The bandit chief just laughed. He ordered his men to get up and go take a closer look at the huge figure of a man, standing with its arms outstretched, in the clearing beyond the tall trees. "Don't you know a statue when you see one?" laughed the chief. Then he touched the statue made of mezcla, a mud cement. As he did so, he saw some writing on its chest. The Spanish words said: "Dig east and west, the way my hands are pointing."

"The treasure!" the bandit chief cried. "Hurry! Get the spades!" And soon the robbers were digging away under the mezcla man's hands. At two, three, and then four feet they found nothing. They were just reaching five feet when they heard loud cries of "Murder! Help! Murder!"

At once, they knew that the ranch workers had returned. The bandits had to get away fast. They rushed out of the bushes, leaped on their horses, and went galloping down the hill. But they were spotted by some of the ranch workers. The workers rode out and quickly captured the bandits.

All the ranch workers climbed the hill and searched around for more robbers. Before long they found the path cut through the bushes. When they discovered the mezcla man and the message on his chest, they ran off to get picks and shovels. "The treasure will belong to the first person who finds it!" shouted one very excited man.

They began digging right then. First, they dug even more deeply into the holes made by the bandits. When they found nothing, they started digging new holes to the east and west, out beyond those started by the bandits.

The digging went on, day after day, for many weeks. Soon people's arms and backs began to hurt badly. They kept on working anyway, until, finally, one tired and angry worker threw down his spade. "Why, there's no gold here," he grumbled. "The old ranchero has tricked us all. I'm sure his fortune is buried where no one can find it. It's lost forever!"

After that, the workers gave up the search. But one man refused to give up. Pedro was sure that he could find the lost treasure. And so, day after day, week after week, and month after month Pedro would come back to the hill each morning and dig and dig until the stars came out.

At first, people admired him. But in time they began to make fun of him. "Well, Pedro!" they would laugh. "Do you need any help to carry all the treasure?"

For a while, the laughter didn't bother Pedro. He would just keep on working hard. But one afternoon, when the heat of the sun was too much to stand, Pedro went to sit in the shade of the mezcla man. Pedro's whole body ached and he had a great thirst. He raised his head to drink some water from a bottle. It was then that he noticed, for the first time, that the statue's mouth was open. It seemed to be laughing at Pedro.

"So, now you too are laughing at me," Pedro cried. "Perhaps the others are right and there is no gold up here. And only I was fool enough to believe the message on your chest!" Of course, the statue didn't answer. It just seemed to keep on laughing at Pedro. This made the pastor so angry that he began to shout. "You old billy goat of a liar! I'll teach you to stop fooling honest people!"

Pedro swung his spade with all his strength. The statue's head came tumbling down. But this didn't satisfy Pedro. He kept hitting at the mezcla man again and again. Finally the spade tore a hole in the stomach of the great statue and hit what sounded like metal. Then, with a loud crash, a great shower of gold and silver coins came rushing out. The brilliant coins spilled over Pedro and soon buried him up to his waist.

Pedro just stood there, laughing and crying, crying and laughing, looking at the dazzling riches all around him. Now he could hardly wait for someone to come climbing up the high hill. Indeed, he could hardly wait for the next person to laugh at him and say, "Well, Pedro! Do you need any help to carry all the treasure?"

THE HEROIC CHIEF
WHOSE NAME
WAS THUNDER....

Vocabulary Preview

commander   [*cum MAN der*]—a person who commands or leads
The general was the *commander* of the army.
dignity   [*DIG ni tee*]—honor and respect
Everyone wants to be treated with *dignity*.
reservation   [*rez er VAY shun*]—land kept for some special use
The young man left the Indian *reservation* to attend
the college in a nearby city.
tourists   [*TOOR ists*]—people who travel for pleasure
The *tourists* traveled hundreds of miles to visit Yellowstone National Park.

Cochise! Geronimo! Crazy Horse! These names and others—Popé, Osceola, Pontiac, Tecumseh—belonged to men famous in American history. They were known as "patriot chiefs." Can you think why? Can you name any other patriot chiefs of the Indian nations?

Joseph, a Nez Percé [*nay PAIR say*] chief, is one of these men. Many legends have grown up around his noble character and great deeds. Read on to discover for yourself why Chief Joseph refused "to sell the bones of his parents," and how he led his people in a desperate race to escape the guns of their enemies.

THE DRUMS WERE BEATING sadly in the night. Old Chief Joseph lay dying in his teepee. After a while, he opened his eyes and smiled at the young man kneeling beside him.

"My son," whispered the old chief. "You must cover your ears when you are asked to sign a treaty selling your home. The white men have their eyes on this land. Never forget my dying words. This country holds your father's body. Never sell the bones of your father and your mother."

The young man looked deeply into his father's eyes and nodded. Then, with a smile on his lips, the old chief died.

The young man was now the leader of his village in the Wallowa Valley in Oregon. There were about six thousand people in the whole Nez Percé nation. They were gathered into villages. Each village had its own chief.

The new chief's real name was Thunder-Traveling-Ever-Higher-Through-the-Mountains, but soon everyone began calling him Chief Joseph. This young husband and father was loved by all his people, and for a short time everything seemed to be going well for him and his village.

251

Then, starting in 1875, white settlers began forcing their way onto Nez Percé land. They even began stealing the Indians' cattle and horses. The Indians didn't want to start a war. Chief Joseph decided to speak to a United States government agent about the problem.

"Never sell the bones of your father and your mother." With these words echoing in his mind, Chief Joseph rode into Fort Lapwai. He was there to meet with General Howard and some other Nez Percé chiefs who were also having trouble with settlers.

The general greeted the colorfully dressed chiefs and listened to their story. Then he shook his head. "I can't help you. The Nez Percés signed a treaty in 1863," he said. "In return for your land, they were given territory on the Lapwai reservation in Idaho. Many Nez Percés are there now. You must take your people there."

Joseph spoke up. He said that neither he nor his father nor any chiefs at this meeting had signed that treaty.

"But the chiefs who did sign it outnumber those who didn't sign it," the general answered. "You must obey the treaty."

Joseph raised his powerful hand. "No," he argued. "Those who signed cannot speak for my people. Each chief must speak for his own village."

Finally, the general became very angry. He slammed his fist down on the table. "I will give you and your people one month to gather your things and get off the land," he roared. "If you are still there after one month, I will send my soldiers to drive you off!"

Joseph's heart was greatly troubled now. He knew that the soldiers far outnumbered his people. He didn't want to see his village wiped out. He thought again of his father's last words. Finally, he said, "I will never agree to any treaty selling my country. But I will lead my people off the land in order to save their lives."

It would have been a wise decision, except that one brave whose father had been killed by a settler became wild with anger when he heard the news. He leaped upon his horse and went riding out of the village with some other men. They raced from farm to farm, killing and scalping people. Then they rode back to the village.

"It's time for war!" they shouted. "There's no way to stop it now. The soldiers are already on their way here!"

Joseph's heart was heavy with sadness. But now there was only one thing he could do. He must lead his people in war—a war for freedom and dignity! With the people in his village, he hurried to White Bird Canyon. "We will wait for the soldiers here," he said.

Two days later, the soldiers arrived. Planning to take the Indians by surprise, they went charging into the canyon. When the soldiers were well inside the canyon, the Indians opened fire from each side of the rocky slopes. The soldiers were shocked. They had fallen into a trap set for them by Chief Joseph—a man who had never fought in a war before.

On that day, guns roared! Horses went spinning around in fright and many soldiers tumbled into the dust! The soldiers who remained alive tried to climb up the sides of the canyon, with angry braves close behind them.

When the braves returned, they danced in victory. Only Joseph had a thoughtful look on his face. "This was only the first battle," he said to himself. "Soon, many more soldiers will come after us. It will be hard for my people." A daring plan was already taking shape in his mind, but he said nothing about it to anyone at this time.

Joseph then led his people forward until they reached the

Clearwater River, where they were soon joined by all of Chief Looking Glass's people. Joseph's problems became even greater, for now he had to keep many more braves, women, children, and old people moving ahead of the soldiers.

Joseph ordered the braves to take cover and wait for the next attack. He knew it would come. He knew the army would come after them. They didn't have to wait long. A group of soldiers suddenly charged. A fierce battle soon raged between three hundred braves and over seven hundred soldiers. Finally, Joseph had to order his people to hurry away.

"We've got them on the run," shouted the soldiers. "Come on, after them!" The soldiers thundered forward after the Indians. But suddenly, to the soldiers' great surprise, a band of braves turned back and charged straight toward them. The braves fought wildly, keeping the soldiers confused until all the other Indians got safely away. Another one of Chief Joseph's plans had worked perfectly!

The warrior chief kept his people moving along until they reached Bitter Root Valley in Montana, where they stopped to rest. There, after his people had beaten off a surprise attack by more soldiers, Joseph and his people pushed on. They were soon attacked by yet another army. Once more, they managed to escape!

Joseph could see that some of his people were looking very tired and frightened. He knew that they needed to have a dream or a goal to keep up their spirits. The wise chief felt the time had come to tell his worried people about his special plan.

"We must head east and then north," he announced. "We must race to the Canadian border. It will be a race for freedom! On the other side of the border we will be safe from the guns of our enemies."

And so the great race began. Joseph hurried up and down

254

the lines of his people, urging them forward, ever forward.

As they hurried through Yellowstone National Park, they captured some tourists—three white men and two white women. "Let's kill them and scalp them," cried one angry brave.

"No!" thundered Chief Joseph. "These people have done us no harm. It would not be right to kill them." And so the grateful tourists were set free.

Joseph kept driving his people onward. After beating off another band of soldiers, the weary Indians crossed the Missouri River and continued on their journey north. Would they reach the Canadian border in time? How many would escape the guns of their enemies and gain their freedom at last?

How happy they were when they saw the Bearpaw Mountains! Joseph lifted his arm and pointed beyond the mountains. "Just thirty miles away is Canada and freedom for us all," he said. "But now you are tired and cold. You must rest. We will camp here tonight."

The moon cast an icy glow over the teepees. Joseph's people were tired but happy. Soon the children began to play games, and the women started singing old songs as they cooked the evening meal. Joseph smiled. How peaceful and right it all seemed.

The chief would not have been so calm if he'd known that a new army, one greater than his people had ever seen before, was approaching from another direction. But now Joseph walked joyfully through the camp with his young daughter.

Suddenly the mighty army came sweeping down like a great storm cloud. The soldiers came thundering right through the middle of the camp, cutting it in two.

"Oh, Father!" screamed Joseph's daughter. "What shall we do?" Joseph didn't answer. He hurled his daughter onto a horse and sent her riding into the hills. Then he turned toward the teepee in which the rest of his family was trapped. He leaped on a horse and went dashing through the enemy lines. Bullets tore holes in his clothing, and his horse was shot out from under him. But he jumped to his feet and raced ahead. His wife was brave enough to meet him at the door of the teepee. "Here is your gun! Fight!" she cried.

At once, Joseph joined his fighting braves. They fought harder than they'd ever fought before, and they succeeded in keeping the soldiers from capturing their camp that night.

When the gray dawn came up, Joseph looked about. Many old people, women, and children lay dead or wounded around him. Upon the rocks dozens of young braves were lying for-ever still. The chief, choked with grief, bowed his head.

The Indians remained trapped in their camp for many days, until one morning Joseph rode out, under a flag of truce, to see the army commander. The two leaders spoke and then Joseph returned to his camp. He told his warriors that they could sur-render and, with the army commander's word, go back to live in peace on a reservation. Or they could, when night fell, make a dash for the Canadian border and freedom. But, explained Joseph, this would mean leaving behind the wounded, the old, and some women and children. The braves knew there was only one decision their noble chief could make. And they watched in sorrow as Joseph rode out once more.

"It is cold and we have no blankets. The little children are freezing to death," Joseph told the army commander. "Some of my people have run away into the hills. They have no blankets or food. I want time to look for all my children. . . . Hear me, my heart is sick and sad. From where the sun now stands, I will fight no more, forever."

Thus the great chief had come to the end of the war trail.

Yet his people looked upon him with love and respect. He was a leader who had fought hard for the rights and liberty of his people. And he had kept his word to his dying father, for he had never signed a treaty selling his country. He had never "sold the bones of his father and his mother."

Joseph, whose real name was Thunder-Traveling-Ever-Higher-Through-the-Mountains, truly lived up to his Indian name. For the legends praising his great deeds are still rising, ever higher, like unending thunder through the mountains, over the plains, and above the cities of this land.

A GRAB BAG OF TALL
TALES *From the West*

In Idaho, a great potato state, they tell this story. A man from the East asked a farmer to sell him two hundred pounds of potatoes. The farmer wouldn't do it. Why? "I won't cut one of my potatoes in half for anybody," he said.

The corn grows really high in Kansas. Once a farmer climbed up a stalk of corn to check its top ears. The corn kept on growing while he was up there. Before the farmer knew it, he was a half mile off the ground. His friends had to send a balloon up to save him.

The smartest burro in the land lived in Virginia City, Nevada. He belonged to a man who had spent years looking for silver. One day the burro finally got tired of waiting for his master to find silver ore. So the burro kicked at some rocks and found the silver for him.

What most people think is a wild storm is just a plain wind to the people of Texas. Folks out there plant iron bars in the cliffs. If the wind bends the bars, Texans go out. If the bars snap in two, Texans stay indoors.

Folks in California say that the sunshine and air in their

state are the best in the land. To prove what they say is true, they tell how a boy rode his bicycle from California to New York to see his sick aunt. His poor aunt was almost dead when he got to her. The doctor said she needed sunshine and fresh air to save her. The boy quickly let the air out of one of his bicycle tires. The California sunshine and fresh air that rushed out saved that woman's life!

A legend of the Paiute Indians says that the huge rocks of different colors and twisted shapes in Bryce Canyon, Utah, were once animals, birds, and lizards. Legends tell us that these once-peaceful animals were changed into the twisted stones as punishment *for beginning to act like people*—by fighting and stealing among themselves.

FOCUSING ON
THE SELECTIONS

Recalling

DIRECTIONS: *Choose the ending that best completes each sentence.*

1. John Henry is remembered for: a) his will to work harder than any machine, b) riding a cyclone, c) telling the first Paul Bunyan tale.
2. In the days of long ago, Americans: a) had no neighborhood stores, b) had no television sets, c) did not swap stories.
3. Harriet Tubman: a) was born in Canada, b) faced great danger, c) never really lived.
4. Joe Magarac stories were probably first told by: a) people from Hungary, b) American Indians, c) people from Canada.
5. Storytellers: a) told only true stories, b) made changes in some stories they told, c) never traveled away from home.
6. A "Liar's Contest" is held: a) nowhere, b) each year in every American town, c) each year in some towns.
7. A tall tale is a story: a) which is always true, b) in which the truth has been stretched very far, c) told only in the West.
8. The greatest steelworker of them all was: a) Joe Magarac, b) Ethan Allen, c) Davy Crockett.
9. It has been said that Paul Bunyan came here from: a) the South, b) Hungary, c) Canada.
10. Tales are told about Pecos Bill: a) working as a lumberjack, b) leading slaves to freedom, c) riding on a cyclone.

Thinking Critically

1. Discuss at least *two* ways in which some legends probably got started.
2. Why was storytelling so popular in days of long ago? Why do you think Americans still enjoy telling the old legends and folk tales?
3. Why are there sometimes different versions of the same story?

4. Without looking at the table of contents in this book, try to name some other characters from the legends and folk tales told in our land.
5. The important characters in some stories that Americans love are not always brave or clever people. In some of these tales, the main characters are funny, or serious, or sly. Can you think of any such characters? (If you can't, put this question aside for a while. After reading this book, you will be able to come back and answer this question with no trouble at all. And that's a fact!)

Recalling

DIRECTIONS: *Match the sentence beginnings in Column A with the sentence endings in Column B.*

A	B
1. The colonists were tired	a. his fist at a redcoat.
2. All people want	b. a British captain.
3. King George planned	c. of paying high taxes.
4. The redcoats had grown	d. the first to die that night.
5. An old man shook	e. like a lobster.
6. Tom became	f. to send a warship.
7. Tom called a dog	g. for speaking against the King.
8. The redcoat looked	h. more troublesome.
9. Crispus was	i. to feel free.
10. The boy's father had been jailed	j. angry and threw down the newspaper.

Thinking Critically

1. How many reasons can you list to explain why the colonists were angry with the English?
2. Why do you think Crispus, more than most people, felt strongly that the colonists should be free to rule themselves?

THE DARING DEED OF ETHAN ALLEN
AND HIS GREEN MOUNTAIN BOYS

Recalling

DIRECTIONS: *Match the sentence beginnings in Column A with the sentence endings in Column B.*

A	B
1. The captain had lost the fort	a. flying upside down.
2. Ethan Allen asked	b. to swim to the fort.
3. Ethan's men had fought	c. a strange voice in the night.
4. The boats looked	d. to a tiny army.
5. Some of Ethan's men were	e. his men to trust him.
6. The two guards heard	f. like floating trees.
7. The flag was	g. the governor of New York Colony.
8. The sleeping soldiers were	h. the captain's sword.
9. Ethan put a sword	i. to the captain's throat.
10. Ethan took	j. in for a surprise.

Thinking Critically

1. Describe a time when you had to wait for an important signal. Tell what the signal was and who sent it. What happened afterward?
2. When movies are being made, "sets" have to be built to show the scenes that are needed. For Ethan Allen's story, one of the sets would have to show a cave. Name at least *five* other sets that would have to be built for a movie based on this story. Try to list the scenes as they appear in the story.
3. People trust a leader who thinks and plans ahead. Mention some things from this story that prove Ethan Allen had thought and planned ahead for the capture of the fort.

266

THE STRANGE ADVENTURE OF
RIP VAN WINKLE

Recalling

DIRECTIONS: *Choose the ending that best completes each sentence.*

1. The old village had been settled by: a) the English, b) the little men, c) the Dutch.
2. The little man was carrying: a) a barrel, b) a sack, c) a chest.
3. Rip found that the noise he'd heard was caused by: a) thunder, b) men playing nine-pins, c) falling rocks.
4. The little men *never*: a) spoke to Rip, b) stopped playing, c) smiled.
5. When Rip woke up, he found he had: a) a white beard, b) no shoes, c) a new gun.
6. When Rip reached his house, he found: a) his dog, b) the roof caved in, c) the door closed.
7. Over the inn door was now a picture of: a) King George, b) George Washington, c) Rip Van Winkle.
8. The story of the ghosts was explained by: a) Rip's daughter, b) Rip's son, c) a wise old man.
9. Rip must have slept: a) the whole night, b) about twelve years, c) about twenty years.
10. Rip learned that he had seen the ghost of: a) Peter Stuyvesant, b) Henry Hudson, c) King George.

Thinking Critically

1. If a man walked into a newspaper office today and could prove that he had been asleep for twenty years, it would probably make the headlines. Make up some headlines that would fit the story of Rip Van Winkle's adventure.
2. Suppose Rip Van Winkle had awakened yesterday after a twenty-year sleep. List some of the important events, discoveries and inventions he would know nothing about.

267

Recalling

DIRECTIONS: *Number the sentences in Group I in the order in which the events happen in the story. The first two have been done for you. Complete Group I and then go on to Group II.*

GROUP I
a. _____ A great noise was heard outside the farmhouse.
b. _____ Brom told about a trick he had played on a friend.
c. __1__ Ichabod gave the class the rest of the day off.
d. _____ Katrina waved to Brom.
e. __2__ Mr. Van Tassel met Ichabod at the door.

GROUP II
a. _____ The guests told ghost stories.
b. _____ Ichabod saw the headless horseman.
c. _____ Brom laughed about the broken pumpkin.
d. _____ The horseman threw its head at Ichabod.
e. _____ Ichabod burst into song.

Thinking Critically

1. Ichabod was sure that Katrina did not like Brom Bones. Do you think Ichabod was right? Find evidence from the story to support your opinion.
2. Why do you suppose Ichabod burst into song when he did? Try to give more than one reason.
3. Was Ichabod the only one who believed in ghosts? Find proof for your answer in the story. Be ready to read your proof to the class.
4. How rich was Ichabod? Find at least *two* facts from the story to support your answer.

268

Recalling

DIRECTIONS: *Number the sentences in Group I in the order in which the events happen in the story. Then go on to Group II.*

GROUP I

a. _____ Johnny gave his horse to Hank.

b. _____ Johnny wanted to keep his secret just for that night.

c. _____ James said he had seen a man talking to a horse.

d. _____ Hank asked Johnny if he had any news to tell.

e. _____ Tess ran out to greet Johnny.

GROUP II

a. _____ Johnny seemed to be talking to a snake in the road.

b. _____ Johnny told the family to go to the fort.

c. _____ The Indian scouts came to the farm.

d. _____ The family heard that the British were coming.

e. _____ Hank was told that he could not work on the farm for a while.

Thinking Critically

1. Why did Johnny keep his "news" to himself for a while? What does this tell us about Johnny?
2. What do you think might have been the reasons Johnny dressed as he did? Try to think of more than one.
3. Why do you think Johnny was called "mad" by some people? Try to think of more than one reason.
4. How does this story show that "He who plants trees loves others besides himself"?
5. What is meant by the sentence, "His kindness had had its own reward"?

Recalling
DIRECTIONS: *Choose the ending that best completes each sentence.*

1. Some people thought that Joe had come from: a) the sea, b) the forests,   c) inside the earth.
2. One woman thought Joe had come from: a) Pittsburgh, b) the stars,   c) the mountains.
3. Joe squeezed steel out between his fingers and made: a) wheels for trains,   b) railroad tracks,   c) beams.
4. Joe could do more work in one hour than: a) dozens of men could do in a day,   b) twenty men could do in a day,   c) hundreds of men could do in a day.
5. The steel mill would have to close because: a) the fires went out in the furnaces,   b) the biggest buyer did not want any more steel,   c) all the iron ore had been used up.
6. Joe wanted to give Pittsburgh: a) its finest steel,   b) a railroad,   c) a new steel mill.
7. Mary said she didn't want Joe to be: a) tired and hungry, b) turned into steel,   c) all alone.
8. The men feared that: a) a house was on fire,   b) a furnace might have blown up,   c) Pete was hurt.
9. The women stayed behind because: a) they had to go home and cook,   b) their husbands didn't want them to get hurt, c) the steel mill had blown up.
10. Pete looked into the great vat because he had: a) heard singing,   b) received a note from Joe,   c) heard Joe calling for him.

Thinking Critically

1. Joe put his duty, dreams and fellow men above his own personal safety. Can you think of other Americans who have done this? Tell the class who these people were, and what they did that caused them to be remembered.
2. Look back in this tale to find clues that help prepare us for the ending of the story.

Recalling

DIRECTIONS: *One of the following words belongs in each sentence below. Place the words in the proper sentences.*

SURGEON, SUPPLIES, SPECIAL, ORGANIZATION, OFFICIALS, WOUNDS, WEARY, WOUNDED, DISASTERS, DETERMINED.

1. Clara wanted a _____ battlefield pass.
2. None of the _____ at the War Department would give Clara a pass.
3. Clara was _____ to find a way to help soldiers on the battle-fields.
4. Clara brought food and other _____ in a wagon.
5. Clara bandaged _____ and fed the troops.
6. Sometimes the _____ men had to wait a long time to see a doctor.
7. Although Clara was _____, she kept on working.
8. Clara acted like a _____ when she removed the bullet from the soldier's face.
9. The Red Cross in Europe was an international _____.
10. Hurricanes and floods are natural _____.

Thinking Critically

1. Clara Barton put service to others above her personal safety and well-being. Can you name other such Americans and tell something about their service to others?
2. What can you tell the class about other famous nurses of America or Europe, and why they are remembered?
3. Clara had many special qualities and abilities. What examples do we have of her determination, kindness, intelligence, and courage?

Recalling

DIRECTIONS: *Number the sentences in Group I in the order in
which the events happen in the story. Then go on to Group II.*

GROUP I

a. _____ Bill splashed through Lake Michigan.
b. _____ Bill heard surprising news from Colorado Cliff.
c. _____ Bill made the captain skip around the boat.
d. _____ The tuna began to swim around in circles.
e. _____ Bill was hit over the head by kidnapers.

GROUP II

a. _____ The fish floated calmly on the sea.
b. _____ Bill threw his belt around the fish.
c. _____ Bill became the best pilot in the harbor.
d. _____ Bill leaped over the rail.
e. _____ The tuna leaped over the ship.

Thinking Critically

1. In this story, Bill was wrong about some of his beliefs. List
   some of the things he was wrong about.
2. At different points in the story, Bill had different feelings. Can
   you tell when and why he felt *puzzled, angry, amused, surprised, homesick?*

272

Recalling

DIRECTIONS: *Choose the ending that best completes each sentence.*

1. Johnny hid in the hole in the tree because: a) he didn't want to work, b) he was cold, c) he was afraid of Paul.
2. Soupy Sim used a canoe to: a) ride around in the soup kettle, b) take Babe for a ride, c) ride over the griddle.
3. The men began to sing at the table because: a) Babe had turned blue, b) they were in a good mood, c) they liked rattlesnake stew.
4. Babe drank up the river because: a) she wanted to see the frogs, b) she wanted to help save Johnny, c) the cooks told her to do it.
5. Everyone liked Johnny because: a) he was the camp's chief cook, b) he was kind, c) he was hiding in a hole in a tree.
6. Babe didn't finish her dessert because: a) she never ate sweet potatoes, b) she wasn't a hog, c) she wanted some apple pie.
7. Johnny woke up at the table because: a) Paul shouted in his ear, b) he smelled the stew, c) he fell off his chair.
8. The log Johnny was sleeping in stopped floating because: a) there was no more water in the river bed, b) it had reached the mill, c) Babe had pulled it to the shore.
9. Cooks skated around with bacon tied to their feet because: a) they were stirring the soup, b) they were greasing the griddle, c) they were catching rattlesnakes.
10. Babe slid down the hill to: a) gather the logs, b) chase Sour-dough Sam, c) break the ice.

Thinking Critically

1. How does this story show that Paul was a "thinking man"?
2. Which parts of this story could never really have happened?

THE FOUNTAIN OF YOUTH

DIRECTIONS: *Match the sentence beginnings in Column A with the sentence endings in Column B.*

A	B
1. The king	a. ran to hide.
2. The young sailors	b. were red, green, orange and blue.
3. The young Indians	c. hoped to find and sell the magic water.
4. Some of the birds' feathers	d. was sending someone else to rule Puerto Rico.
5. One young Indian in Florida	e. ran from the ship to Ponce's house.
6. Sharp stones	f. dropped from their backs.
7. The leaves of the trees	g. drew pictures in the dirt.
8. The men's packs	h. cut through the men's worn-out boots.
9. A monument honoring Ponce	i. were bright yellow.
10. The King's messenger	j. was built in San Juan.

Thinking Critically

1. One day a lady screamed because someone told her there was a spider on the stove. The lady had jumped to a conclusion. She didn't know that the old-fashioned word for frying pan is "spider." In the story we have just read, Ponce's sailors jumped to some conclusions. Mention two of these conclusions.
2. In this story, we read that the leaves *blazed like gold.* Try to make some comparisons of your own. Supply two sentence endings for each of the following: a. The ocean was as blue as _____. b. His hair was as white as _____. c. The stones cut like _____. d. The ocean's waves leaped like _____.
3. Do you think Ponce de Leon was foolish to think there was a Fountain of Youth? How many modern people still search for things to make them look young again? What are some of the things you have seen advertised? Do you think such people are foolish? Why, or why not?

Recalling

DIRECTIONS: *Match the sentence beginnings in Column A with the sentence endings in Column B.*

A	B
1. The children made up their minds	a. changed his mind at the gate.
2. The men and women	b. not to eat breakfast.
3. Betty's greatest wish was	c. put out all the fires.
4. Betty stopped once	d. tore the flower from Betty's hair.
5. A bird swooped	e. to save her friends.
6. The Indian braves	f. out of the sky.
7. General Zane suddenly	g. to pick a flower.
8. A swift arrow	h. wondered what was in the blanket.
9. The keg rolled	i. wanted to sneak out of the fort.
10. One of the general's men	j. out of the blanket.

Thinking Critically

1. Have you ever had to run a long distance to get somewhere in a hurry? Think about why you were running. Describe your thoughts and feelings as you ran along.
2. We can describe many exciting "pictures" from this story. But let's pretend that we are going to tape-record this legend as a play. What *sounds* might we put on the tape?
3. Betty and the other children in this story were brave. Tell the class about another brave child you know or have read about.
4. Do you think General Zane did the right thing in allowing Betty to go for the powder? Why, or why not? Why did he try to stop her at the last minute?

Recalling

DIRECTIONS: *One of the following words belongs in each sentence below. Place the words in the proper sentences.*

SPIRITS, STREAM, BRIGHTLY, BEAST, SHARP, SCRATCHED, ESCAPE, EXCEPT, BERRIES, BLUSH.

1. Daniel began to smile and _____ while he stood talking to the girl.
2. Daniel had a _____ sense of hearing.
3. The girl wanted to pick some _____ for a pie.
4. The girl's parents were building a cabin near a _____.
5. The night was still, _____ for the sound of footsteps.
6. The girl's green eyes shone _____.
7. Daniel _____ his head, wondering about the sound he'd heard.
8. He feared that a wild _____ might be hiding behind the trees.
9. Daniel wondered if the stories about ghosts and _____ could be true.
10. He knew that he couldn't _____ from what was hiding in the grove of trees.

Thinking Critically

1. What safety measures might the girl have taken to make sure that she would not get lost in the woods? Try to think of more than one.
2. Have you ever been lost in the woods or somewhere else? Tell the class how you felt and how you finally got home.
3. Can you think of at least *three* reasons Daniel might have had for killing bears?

DANIEL BOONE, FIRST DETECTIVE OF THE OLD FRONTIER

Recalling

DIRECTIONS: *Number the sentences in Group I in the order in which the events happen in the story. Then go on to Group II.*

GROUP I

a. _____ The girls saw an Indian swimming beside the canoe.

b. _____ Daniel began to follow an old Indian trail.

c. _____ The girls went to catch frogs near the river.

d. _____ The Indians had been hiding in a tree.

e. _____ Daniel saw the canoe stuck against some rocks.

GROUP II

a. _____ The sound of a little stream helped guide Daniel home.

b. _____ The Indian brave thought he heard a forest spirit.

c. _____ Daniel saw that the tracks went off the narrow path.

d. _____ The sound of laughter echoed through the woods.

e. _____ Daniel gave a fierce yell and leaped out into the open.

Thinking Critically

1. Daniel was like a detective. He used clues to help him solve his problem. Can you name some clues he used?
2. What kinds of chores do you think pioneer boys and girls did for their families? Make two lists, one for the pioneer boys and one for the pioneer girls.

MIKE FINK AND THE RIVER PIRATES

Recalling

DIRECTIONS: *Choose the ending that best completes each sentence.*

1. Aurelia wanted Mike to take her to: a) Ohio,   b) Pittsburgh,
   c) see the pirates.
2. Tall Ned was: a) Aurelia's brother,   b) a pirate,   c) a captain.
3. The pirates were afraid to tell Camilla that Ned: a) had escaped,   b) had taken their money,   c) had been shot.
4. Mike knew the pirates were on their way because: a) Ned
   had told him,   b) Aurelia had told him,   c) Camilla's daughter
   had told him.
5. Mike shot holes through: a) a big horn,   b) the sails of the
   pirate ship,   c) the Jolly Roger.
6. Mike hid his red feather: a) to keep it safe,   b) to fool the
   pirates,   c) to give to an Indian chief.
7. Camilla didn't know: a) his hut was on fire,   b) his child was
   following him,   c) where Aurelia had been hidden.
8. Ned led Mike: a) into a burning hut,   b) to Pittsburgh,   c)
   to the pirates' hideout.
9. Mike cried when: a) he thought Aurelia was dead,   b) he
   saw the creature in white in the woods,   c) the *Lightfoot*
   sank.
10. Captain Camilla: a) killed Ned,   b) turned over a boat,   c)
    set fire to the pirates' cave.

Thinking Critically

1. Why do you suppose the people of the early 1800's depended
   so much on riverboats and on the men who piloted them?
2. Can you find evidence that proves that Mike was both *clever*
   and *kind?*

278

Recalling

DIRECTIONS: *Choose the ending that best completes each sentence.*

1. Harriet served as: a) a sheriff,   b) a nurse,   c) a postmaster.
2. Harriet led her brothers to: a) Maryland,   b) the sheriff's office,   c) Canada.
3. Harriet was afraid that her mother would: a) push supplies through the door,   b) send for the sheriff,   c) shout for joy.
4. Jacob received: a) a package,   b) a letter,   c) a poster.
5. The reward for Harriet's capture was: a) four thousand dollars,   b) fourteen thousand dollars,   c) forty thousand dollars.
6. The men looking for Harriet's brothers knew her father was: a) honest,   b) lying,   c) a conductor on the railroad.
7. One stop on the railroad was: a) the sheriff's office,   b) Ohio, c) a fodder house.
8. The person who wanted to stop for a rest was: a) a thirteen-year-old girl,   b) a huge man,   c) Ben.
9. Harriet became strong from: a) carrying people,   b) working on a farm,   c) sweeping the front steps.
10. John caught up with the others: a) just before dawn,   b) just at dawn,   c) just after dawn.

Thinking Critically

1. Some people can think very quickly when a problem comes up. Name at least three people in this story and tell how each one of them acted quickly to solve a problem.
2. Describe the Underground Railroad. What was its purpose? Why was this a good name for it?
3. What do you know about the real Moses? Why was Harriet Tubman called "the Moses of her people"?

JOHN HENRY AND THE MONSTER

DIRECTIONS: *Choose the ending that best completes each sentence.*

1. John Henry wanted to go to: a) the city, b) California, c) West Virginia.
2. John Henry wanted to: a) have a long rest, b) run a railroad train, c) help dig the Big Bend Tunnel.
3. John Henry rocked his son to sleep: a) in a cradle of wood, b) in his big hand, c) in his arms.
4. The monster was really: a) a big tunnel, b) a steam drill, c) the boss of the camp.
5. The man from the city said that if John Henry won the contest: a) the boss could have the steam drill for nothing, b) the steam drill would be exploded into bits, c) the boss should give John a raise.
6. Polly began to: a) sing for John Henry, b) shout at the crowd, c) shout at her husband.
7. John Henry hit the drill so hard that he: a) broke the hammers, b) wore out the heads of the hammers, c) had to get a new drill.
8. Some men threw pails of cold water to: a) keep John Henry's hammers from melting away, b) wet the steam drill, c) cool John Henry off.
9. The boss of the camp: a) did the drilling that day, b) did the measuring that day, c) took the baby to the house that day.
10. Polly had tears in her eyes because she thought: a) the noise might wake up the baby, b) John Henry needed rest and might hurt himself, c) the boss might have to pay for the machine.

Thinking Critically

1. Polly's fears became stronger and stronger as the contest went on. Find and discuss lines that show this is so.
2. Why do you think the people wanted to see John beat the steam drill? Why do you think most people would like to see a man beat a machine?

Recalling

DIRECTIONS: *One of the following words belongs in each sentence below. Place the words in the proper sentences.*

EXPRESS, ENGINEER, FIREMAN, FOREMAN, SUPPLIES, SPARKS, WHISTLE, BOWED, WRONG, WARN.

1. The _____ said the driver of Number 638 was sick.
2. Sim Webb was the _____ on the Cannonball.
3. Train 638 was carrying some _____ that were needed.
4. Casey Jones was a famous _____.
5. Rockets were used to _____ of danger.
6. _____ flew up from the tracks as the Cannonball screeched down the hill.
7. A train had switched to the _____ track in the dark.
8. Casey and Sim could hear a _____ coming from another train.
9. The men stumbled up to the wreck of the Cannonball _____.
10. The men took off their caps and _____ their heads.

Thinking Critically

1. Casey did many things to try to prevent an accident that night. Name at least *three* of these things.
2. Sim was a good friend. Can you point out *two* things he did that proved this?
3. Casey is remembered for his great act of heroism. Can you tell the class about a hero or heroine you have read about or know from real life?

THE COURAGE OF "BIRD WOMAN"

Recalling

DIRECTIONS: *Match the sentence beginnings in Column A with the sentence endings in Column B.*

A	B
1. Thomas Jefferson	a. kept a record of plant life seen along the way.
2. Sacajawea	
3. The French interpreter	b. bought the Louisiana Territory.
4. A war party	c. was Sacajawea's brother.
5. The great chief of the Shoshones	d. sold the Louisiana Territory.
	e. was named for Sacajawea.
6. A river	f. were expecting Lewis and Clark's party.
7. The ocean	
8. Lewis	g. stole Sacajawea from her village as a child.
9. The Shoshones	
10. France	h. was Sacajawea's husband.
	i. asked to adopt her sister's child.
	j. was called the water that is always salty.

Thinking Critically

1. It is said that Sacajawea had a fine memory. It is also said that she was *brave, intelligent, kind* and *strong*. Find sentences in the story that help to prove that each of these things said about the Indian princess was true.

2. In this story you read about a famous American woman. Can you identify the brave American women listed below? Tell all you can about each of them.

    Clara Barton   Barbara Fritchie   Helen Keller

Recalling

DIRECTIONS: *Choose the ending that best completes each statement.*

1. Many Americans felt that Texas belonged to the United States because: a) three-fourths of the settlers in Texas were Americans, b) Texas was a republic, c) Mexico had sold it to the United States.

2. The messenger sent to the Alamo by Santa Anna hurried back because: a) Santa Anna called him, b) he was frightened, c) Travis rode out after him.

3. Colonel Travis was filled with both joy and sadness because: a) he had escaped to the nearest fort, b) Davy had brought him a letter from home, c) his men had promised to fight to the last breath.

4. Bee-hunter didn't seem to know where he was because: a) he had been shot, b) smoke from the cannons filled his room, c) he got lost while searching for Old Pirate.

5. Jim Bowie was unhappy because: a) Colonel Travis didn't like him, b) he had lost his knife, c) he couldn't get out of bed to fight.

6. Davy's family let him go to Texas so he could: a) get a fresh supply of food for them, b) help the Texans fight for freedom, c) rescue Jim Bowie.

7. Santa Anna probably had his army march toward the Alamo in order to: a) fill the people in the fort with terror, b) surrender to Colonel Travis, c) punish the Americans who refused to settle in Texas.

8. Old Pirate had tried to get to another fort in order to: a) lead Santa Anna there, b) get help for the people in the Alamo, c) get a doctor for Bee-hunter.

9. Davy ran out of the fort in order to: a) find his horse, b) capture Santa Anna, c) help Old Pirate.

10. General Castillon brought Davy and the other prisoners to

Santa Anna in order to: a) have them shot, b) save their lives, c) make them colonels.

Thinking Critically

1. In this story, there were times when Davy had different feelings. Tell when and why Davy felt *embarrassed, sorrowful, angry.*
2. Compare this story to the one called "Betty Zane, the Youngest General." In what ways are the stories alike? For instance, what were the people in both stories trying to do? What events in one story remind you of events in the other story? Are the endings alike or different? Explain.

ANNIE OAKLEY, CHAMPION SHARPSHOOTER

Recalling

DIRECTIONS: *One of the following words belongs in each sentence below. Place the words in the proper sentences.*

AMAZING, ASSISTANT, DELIGHTED, DESTROYED, ENTERTAIN, ENTERTAINER, MATCH, MEDALS, SHATTER, SUPPORT.

1. Annie shot and sold birds to help _____ the family.
2. Clay pigeons were hurled up at the shooting _____.
3. The judge watched the bullet _____ the target.
4. Frank became Annie's manager and _____ in show business.
5. Annie, a great _____, thrilled audiences with her sharpshooting.
6. The crowds thought her sharpshooting tricks were _____.
7. Annie was _____ to join *Buffalo Bill's Wild West Show*.
8. Annie liked to _____ audiences in America and Europe.
9. Some kings and queens gave her _____ and other presents.
10. Some of the hurt horses had to be _____ after the train wreck.

Thinking Critically

1. Although Annie was born in the East (in Greenville, Ohio), why is she considered an important character in the folk lore of the West? How does she represent the West?
2. Why might this story be called a love story?
3. How did she use her gift as a sharpshooter to help her family, other people, and her country?
4. Who are some present-day entertainers who use their gifts to help other people?

Recalling

DIRECTIONS: *Number the sentences in Group I in the order in which the events happen in the story. Then go on to Group II.*

GROUP I

a. _____ The bugler called the men together.

b. _____ The general broke his regiment up into three groups.

c. _____ Custer saw a terrible sight.

d. _____ Custer pinned a silver star to his scarf.

e. _____ Indians stormed down the hills.

GROUP II

a. _____ Custer threw away his gun and pulled out his sword.

b. _____ Rain-in-the-Face would not let an Indian take Custer's scalp.

c. _____ Rain-in-the-Face leaped like a wolf.

d. _____ Some men fought the Indians hand to hand.

e. _____ Rain-in-the-Face jumped down from his horse.

Thinking Critically

1. Each of the two great warriors set up a trap for the other. Tell all you can about each of these traps. Perhaps you will want to draw a diagram on the blackboard or on paper to make what you say clear.

2. There are ways of being a *good loser*, and there are ways of being a *good winner*. Make a list of examples for each of these.

Recalling

DIRECTIONS: *One of the following words belongs in each sentence below. Place the words in the proper sentences.*

WEAVING, WAVING, JOKED, JACKET, POLITE, PARTNER, SPORT, STRETCH, SNORTED, STRANGER.

1. Pride began _____ in and out of the herd.
2. Jim laughed at the long hair of the _____.
3. The Westerner felt that buffalo shouldn't be hunted for _____.
4. Jim bragged and _____ too much.
5. George was very _____ to the hunter.
6. William F. Cody was _____ his hat in farewell.
7. The men saw the buffalo on a _____ of flat land.
8. The hunter's _____ was waiting for him at their camp.
9. The buffalo _____ and moved around.
10. Jim's fancy hunting _____ was covered with dust.

Thinking Critically

1. Name at least *four* things Pride did that prove the title of this story is a good one.
2. Do you think Jim got what he deserved? Why? Do you know another tale about someone who got just what was coming to him? Tell the class about it.

Recalling

DIRECTIONS: *Choose the ending that best completes each sentence.*

1. Bill didn't cry when he fell out of the wagon because: a) he saw a lion, b) he thought it was a game, c) his brothers and sisters were laughing at him.
2. The pups made Bill their chief because: a) he beat them up, b) he had no tail, c) his ears were pointy.
3. The lion leaped on Bill because: a) it wanted to teach the pups to howl, b) it was jealous of Bill, c) it wanted to take the lasso.
4. Bill thought the cowboy he'd rescued was a coyote because: a) the cowboy howled like a coyote, b) the cowboy rode a lion, c) Bill hadn't seen a fellow human being for so long.
5. The rattlesnakes crawled over to Bill because: a) Bill had whistled to them, b) the bull was chasing Bill, c) they wanted to learn to howl.
6. Bill taught the cowboys to: a) make and use snake lassos, b) tame wild horses, c) ride cyclones.
7. Bill didn't run to hide from the cyclone because: a) he hadn't been told to run, b) he had never seen a cyclone before, c) he always rode cyclones.
8. The cyclone tore up houses and trees to: a) show its strength, b) chase the rattlesnakes out of Texas, c) build a house for Bill.
9. Bill let the cyclone go because: a) it threw Bill off its back, b) it gave Bill a ten-gallon hat, c) it promised to be nice to people.
10. Bill said the cyclone had: a) earned a sheriff's star, b) become the coyote chief, c) cried itself out.

Thinking Critically

1. Name the many things Bill tamed and tell how he tamed each of them.

2. Bill was lost, and yet he managed to stay alive and take good care of himself. Discuss other stories in which someone was lost and had to learn to make the best of things in his new home. (Think of books you have read and of movies and television programs you have seen.)

THE STRANGE ARMIES FROM THE SKY

Recalling

DIRECTIONS: *Fill in the blank space in each sentence. Choose your answers from these action words:* TENDING, ATTACKING, DASHING, GATHER, PLAYING, CLOSED, STARED, FOUGHT, RECEIVED, COVERED.

1. The farmers were _____ their crops.
2. The boys were _____ a game.
3. When Joseph _____ his eyes, the sun was shining.
4. Father came _____ out of the barn.
5. Father told the family to _____ all the blankets in the house.
6. The family _____ to save some of their crops.
7. The locusts _____ the fields for miles around.
8. The sea gulls began _____ the locust army.
9. The sea-gull army rose as if it had _____ a signal.
10. Father _____ at the birds until they were out of sight.

Thinking Critically

1. Locusts can ruin a farmer's crops. A cyclone can also ruin crops. Can you think of *three* other ways in which crops can be ruined? What can be done about them?
2. We have learned how locusts may ruin a farmer's hard work. What other insects can be harmful to crops or men? Can you think of any insects that are helpful to man?
3. List at least *three* words that tell how the farmer and his family might have *felt* while they were fighting the locusts. List at least *three* words that tell how the farmer and his family might have felt after the sea gulls were gone. Discuss why you chose each of the words.

Recalling

DIRECTIONS: *Choose the ending that best completes each sentence.*

1. Febold had just come from: a) England, b) Canada, c) Sweden.
2. The people in New York wanted to make Febold: a) a policeman, b) the mayor, c) a fireman.
3. Febold reached Nebraska in: a) just three hundred steps, b) a few giant steps, c) just five hundred steps.
4. Along the riverbanks were: a) cottonwood trees, b) cornstalks, c) willow trees.
5. The chief of the insects was as big as: a) a tree, b) a soup kettle, c) three cows.
6. The insects wanted Febold's: a) horse, b) kettle, c) land.
7. Febold had to hide: a) under his bed, b) under his soup kettle, c) in a nearby state.
8. Mr. Johnson was carried: a) in Febold's pocket, b) under Febold's arm, c) by the chief of the insects.
9. Over the corn fields were stripes of: a) sunshine, b) rain, c) snow.
10. Syrup was washed out of the: a) cornstalks, b) sugar cane, c) popcorn balls.

Thinking Critically

1. Why do you think the people wanted Febold to stay in New York? Give more than one reason.
2. Have you ever known or read about a person who seemed to be able to solve almost any problem? Tell the class about this person and about one of the great problems he or she solved.
3. We read that Febold's sugar cane grew tall in one day. Can you think of other tales in which crops grew up to great size or with great speed?

4. We read that the popcorn ball was "invented" by the striped weather. Make up a "tall story" (either alone or working with the class) about how one of the following was invented: THE PEPPERMINT CANE, THE PRETZEL, THE GUM DROP, PEANUT BRITTLE.

Recalling

DIRECTIONS: *Number the sentences in Group I in the order in which the events happen in the story. Then go on to Group II.*

GROUP I

a. _____ Jim wanted to bet that Star would win the race.

b. _____ Jim wanted to bet that his friend's wife would not be cured.

c. _____ Jim wanted to bet he'd catch the man who had cheated him.

d. _____ Jim wanted to bet on which bird would fly off first.

e. _____ Jim wanted to bet on his frog.

GROUP II

a. _____ The stranger filled Jim's frog with gunshot.

b. _____ Star won the race.

c. _____ Jim said he might have a parrot in the box.

d. _____ Jim ran to find a frog for the stranger.

e. _____ Jim dashed down the road after the stranger.

Thinking Critically

1. In this story we learn that Jim liked to bet with strangers. What do you think Jim's reasons were for this?

2. Sometimes a person plans a trick, but the joke turns out to be on him. How did this happen to Jim? Do you think he got what he deserved? Why or why not?

Recalling

DIRECTIONS: *Choose the ending that best completes each sentence.*

1. The boys didn't call the police at once because: a) Don's father told them not to, b) they didn't want to make fools of themselves, c) Doctor Storm told them to call the Air Force.
2. Mother turned off the radio that night because: a) the news about the strange objects frightened her, b) she wanted Don to tell her about the objects he had seen, c) the police were at the door.
3. Don couldn't sleep, so: a) he went out looking for flying saucers, b) he called up Doctor Storm, c) he decided to get things ready for the next day.
4. The coach asked the boys to leave the court because: a) they were talking about the strange objects to everyone, b) they had come to school late, c) they kept crashing into the other boys.
5. The boys went to the plant on Rowe Street to: a) practice basketball, b) see Doctor Storm, c) borrow long white coats.
6. Don didn't show the gray stuff to Doctor Storm because: a) Don thought the scientist was not telling all he knew, b) the Air Force officer had taken it away, c) Doctor Storm had not wanted to see it.
7. Doctor Storm went to Don's apartment because: a) he had stolen Don's key, b) he wanted to steal the web, c) Don had asked him to be there.
8. The Air Force officer took the web: a) to have it tested, b) to burn it quickly, c) to give it to Doctor Storm.
9. The police had come to Don's house because: a) some neighbors had called them, b) Don's mother had called them, c) the police had seen a man climbing in a back window.
10. The boys took a different route to the center for months because: a) Doctor Storm told them to, b) they were afraid to pass the place where they had seen the strange objects, c) they kept following Doctor Storm.

Thinking Critically

1. Do you think the boys did the right thing in not telling their parents and the police about the strange objects right away? Why or why not?

2. *Without rereading any part of the story,* try to describe the object that Don and Ted saw hovering in the air. Now look back in the story to see if your description is completely right. If you find your description and the one in the story don't match exactly, what should this tell you about one of the ways in which legends grow and change?

THE SEARCH FOR THE RANCHERO'S LOST TREASURE

Recalling

DIRECTIONS: *Number the sentences in Group I in the order in which the events happen in the story. Then go on to Group II.*

GROUP I

a. _____The bandits thought they saw the ranchero's ghost.

b. _____The ranch workers went off to a wedding fiesta.

c. _____The bandits began digging under the mezcla man's hands.

d. _____The bandits chopped up the furniture.

e. _____The bandits rode around the ranch, looking for clues.

GROUP II

a. _____The ranch workers began to laugh at Pedro.

b. _____Pedro felt that the mezcla man seemed to be laughing at him.

c. _____The ranch workers ran off to get picks and shovels.

d. _____Pedro could hardly wait for the next person to ask if he needed some help.

e. _____Pedro hit the statue with a spade.

Thinking Critically

1. Does the ending of the story satisfy you? Why, or why not?
2. What other stories do you know about lost treasure or treasure hunts? Include stories you have heard, read, or seen on television or at the movies.
3. In what ways has treasure hunting changed since the old days? Think in terms of modern science and new equipment.

Recalling

DIRECTIONS: *Choose the ending that best completes each sentence.*

1. Joseph went to the fort to: a) declare war, b) get help, c) sign a treaty.
2. Joseph led his people off the land to: a) attack settlers, b) go to a reservation, c) save their lives.
3. One brave scalped settlers because: a) his father had been killed, b) he wanted their horses, c) Joseph had ordered it.
4. Joseph went to the canyon to: a) meet Chief Looking Glass, b) prepare an ambush, c) hide until it was safe to go home.
5. Joseph wanted to take his people to Canada because: a) it was their homeland, b) the hunting was better there, c) they'd be free and safe there.
6. Joseph had the tourists set free because: a) they begged for mercy, b) they were all women, c) they'd done no harm.
7. Joseph felt calm and happy, so: a) he sang old songs, b) he took a walk, c) he sat before his teepee.
8. Joseph put his child on a horse to: a) send her to safety, b) teach her to ride, c) lead her into Canada.
9. Joseph's wife risked her life to: a) rescue her daughter, b) help a wounded brave, c) give Joseph his gun.
10. Joseph surrendered because: a) all his braves were dead, b) his people were suffering terribly, c) he was wounded.

Thinking Critically

1. How does Joseph's story remind you of any others you have heard, or read, or seen on television or at the movies?
2. Why might Joseph easily stand as a symbol for all or many of the other patriot chiefs?

BRINGING THE STORIES TOGETHER

1. When a famous man dies, people begin telling many interesting stories about him. Sometimes these stories are based on the true experiences of the man. Often they are based on what some people *believe* to have been the man's experiences. As the years go by, these tales grow and change as they are passed on from person to person. They become *legends.*

   How, then, is historical fact different from legend? Why do you think Americans enjoy reading legends, even when they know that the stories aren't completely true?

2. You know that some legends are "tall tales" about people who really lived, while others are about "made-up" characters. Which major characters in this book were people who really lived? How can you find proof that you are right?

3. Paul Bunyan and Febold Feboldson are sometimes called "tamers (or masters) of the land." Can you tell why? Why do you think Americans have made these characters so big and so clever?

4. What stories or parts of stories made you laugh most? What characters did you think were funny? Why were they humorous?

5. What stories or parts of stories made you feel sad? Why were they sad, in your opinion?

6. Some stories or parts of stories in this book have a moral, or lesson, they teach the reader. Usually this moral can be put into a single sentence, often a well-known saying or *proverb.* The moral of "Johnny Appleseed" might be said to be "Kindness begets kindness."

   To what stories would you apply the following sayings?

   a) "Don't judge a book by its cover."
   b) "All that glitters is not gold."
   c) "He who laughs last, laughs best."
   d) "Fortune favors the bold."

   What other proverbs can you think of that fit one or more of the stories? (You may use old sayings, or make up your own.)

7. Many characters in these stories were very brave. Starting with bravery, match the following qualities with characters from the stories you have read:
   - a) bravery
   - b) cleverness
   - c) foolishness
   - d) wisdom
   - e) boastfulness
   - f) cruelty
   - g) loyalty
   - h) greediness
   - i) honesty
   - j) kindness
   - k) love of family

STORY THEATER

BETTY ZANE, THE YOUNGEST GENERAL

(A play for radio or tape recorder)

CAST OF CHARACTERS

Announcer	Third Woman
Narrator	Bright Cloud
Mother	Brave Eagle
Boy	Swift Deer
General	Fourth Woman
Major	Fifth Woman
First Young Man	Third Young Man
Second Young Man	
Betty	Voices of Settlers
First Woman	Voices of Indians
Second Woman	

ANNOUNCER: Good day to all our listeners. Our class is happy to present a play based on a daring event from the life of Betty Zane. Betty was a girl who was willing to risk her life to help her friends. She and some other settlers were trapped in a fort. It was on land that is now part of Wheeling, West Virginia. The British had urged the Indians to attack the fort. The story takes place during the time of the Revolutionary War. What was Betty's daring plan to save the fort? Let's go back through the years to find out.

NARRATOR: Fort Henry has been under Indian attack all night. The men and women in the fort are worn out. For hours they have been putting out the fires caused by flaming arrows. Now it is dawn, and the fighting has stopped for a while. Everything is still. The children are creeping out of their hiding places. They can see the arrows stuck in the walls and smell the thick smoke from the fires. It hangs above their heads like a gray cloud.

BOY: Are they gone, Mother? Are we safe now?

MOTHER: Come. There's no time to speak of that. You must have some breakfast.

BOY: No, Mother. The boys and girls know that supplies are low. We have decided not to eat breakfast. That will save lots of food.

GENERAL: Do you hear that, men? Even the children are helping now. I'm sure we'll win this fight! All we have to do is hold off the Indians for a few more hours. Help should reach us by then.

MAJOR: A few more hours, General? We can't hold on for even one more hour. We're in real trouble now! We need gunpowder, and there's barely a pinch left in the whole fort.

GENERAL: That's true, Major. If only I could think of a plan. But wait! I've just remembered something. There's a whole keg of gunpowder in my cabin!

VOICES: A whole keg! That might be enough! We may be saved!

MAJOR: You say the powder's in your cabin? How can that help us? Your cabin is out there, past the Indians. It's more than a hundred feet from the walls of the fort!

FIRST YOUNG MAN: That needn't stop us! General, let me sneak out. I'll get the powder!

GENERAL: No, you'd be shot down before you were halfway there.

SECOND YOUNG MAN: Let me go. I'm a swift runner!

GENERAL: Quiet! We have only eighteen men left in the entire fort. There are women and children to think of. Not one man can be spared. We must try to hold the fort without the powder.

BETTY: (*after a short pause*) Not one man can be spared, that's true, Father. But a girl may be spared. Let me go for the keg.

GENERAL: What, Betty? Let you go out among the Indians? They'd shoot you on sight!

BETTY: I'm your child. Doesn't that almost make me a soldier too?

GENERAL: I can't believe my ears, daughter. You've always been so afraid of the woods and the Indians.

BETTY: You *must* let me go. I can't fire a gun like a soldier, but I can run as fast as one. Please let me try. It's our only chance.

GENERAL: (*with a sigh*) You are right, my child. The powder might save a great many lives. (*he pauses*) All right men, open the gate.

(*sounds of a gate squeaking open*)

BETTY: Good-by, Father. Wish me luck.

GENERAL: No, stop! Stop! I've changed my mind! I can't let you go!

302

MAJOR: It's too late, General. She's slipped out of the fort already. (*sounds of the gate squeaking closed and slamming*)

FIRST WOMAN: Poor child! She can't possibly make it. We should never have let her go.

SECOND WOMAN: Look through the cracks in the logs! Betty isn't even running to the cabin. She acts as if she were out for a Sunday stroll!

FIRST WOMAN: Why aren't the Indians shooting arrows at her?

SECOND WOMAN: Maybe they're as surprised as we are at her actions.

THIRD WOMAN: Look! Look! Betty's stooping to pick a flower!

FIRST WOMAN: Yes, and she's putting it in her hair!

THIRD WOMAN: The poor child. What can she be thinking of?

GENERAL: Thank heavens! She's reached the cabin, and she's going inside. I wonder what the Indians are thinking about all this? (*a slight pause; then the sound of rustling leaves*)

BRIGHT CLOUD: Brave Eagle, why didn't you let us shoot the girl?

BRAVE EAGLE: Because, Bright Cloud, I am puzzled. Maybe this is a trick. Let us wait to see what she will do next.

SWIFT DEER: There she is. She's coming out of the cabin now. She has something wrapped in a blanket.

BRAVE EAGLE: Put down your bow, Swift Deer. We will watch this girl for a few more moments.

BRIGHT CLOUD: She must have clothes in that bundle.

BRAVE EAGLE: No, she would not risk her life for clothes. She must be carrying food, or a child.

SWIFT DEER: Look! A bird has startled her. See? She has dropped the bundle. But look what is rolling out of the blanket! It's a keg of gunpowder! We have been tricked!

BRIGHT CLOUD: Quick! She's picking up the keg and starting to run!

BRAVE EAGLE: Get her! Get her! Don't let her escape! (*loud whoops and war cries of many Indians; sounds of arrows whistling through the air*)

BETTY: Oh! They've hit the keg with an arrow. I've got to make it back to the fort quickly. Will I never get there? (*sounds of more arrows*) They've shot the flower from my hair! My legs —they're growing weaker. I'm starting to feel dizzy. Oh, no! I mustn't faint now! I mustn't! The fort is just ahead.

GENERAL: Faster, Betty! Faster! The gate is open! Run!

MANY VOICES: Hurry, Betty! Run! Run!
(*sound of the gate slamming shut; then the sound of arrows striking the closed gate*)
GENERAL: My daughter! You're safe! You're safe!
FOURTH WOMAN: And we're safe too! Betty has saved our lives!
MAJOR: (*shouting*) Three cheers for General Betty, the bravest soldier of them all!
MANY VOICES: (*shouting loudly*) Three cheers for General Betty! Hurrah! Hurrah!
BETTY: Oh! I'm out of breath. I must lie down for a few moments.
FIFTH WOMAN: You've earned a good rest, my dear. Come, I'll help you to your room.
GENERAL: Men, the Indians will soon be attacking again. Open the keg of powder. That's it. Take all you need.
MANY MEN: Pass some this way . . . Here, I'll take some . . . Me too . . . We'll be ready for the Indians this time!
GENERAL: And I think we can hold the fort for more than just a few hours.
SECOND YOUNG MAN: We will, thanks to Betty, the youngest general!
FIRST YOUNG MAN: That's a good name for her, all right.
FIFTH WOMAN: General Zane, she's sound asleep.
GENERAL: So soon?
FIFTH WOMAN: Yes. The poor child fell fast asleep as soon as her head touched the pillow. And she was smiling in her sleep.
GENERAL: Smiling? I wonder how she could smile after such a terrible experience.
THIRD YOUNG MAN: Perhaps she was remembering our cheer for her: "Three cheers for General Betty!" I'm sure it's a memory that will live in her heart for a long, long time.
VOICES OF INDIANS: (*whoops and war cries coming from far away; then they grow louder and louder*)
GENERAL: Listen, my friends. The battle has started again.
VOICES OF INDIANS: (*very loud war cries; then they fade out as the narrator begins to speak*)
NARRATOR: Yes, the battle had begun again. But because of Betty Zane's daring action, the settlers were able to hold out until help reached them that evening. Her brave deed helped to bring the early fighters for liberty a step closer to winning independence and freedom for all. . . .

304

ANNOUNCER: Our class hopes that you have enjoyed the play that was just presented. We thank you for listening, and we wish you a good day.

Now that you have presented the play in this book, see if your class can write its own play. You may write it about one of the legends in the book or about any other tale that you like. When your play is finished, present it in class or record it on a tape recorder.

How well can you pantomime? For example, without speaking or using any "props," can you make people *believe* that you are climbing a ladder or painting a picture? Here are a few suggestions for pantomimes you might want to try:

1. You are walking through the woods. Suddenly you hear a strange sound. You stand still because you are afraid that a bear might be nearby. After a while, you decide that you must have been hearing things. Relaxed, you start off again. All of a sudden, you hear the strange sound again. This time you think the bear may be directly in back of you. You freeze with fear.
2. You think you hear singing. You climb a ladder to a narrow platform. You try to look straight down into a huge vat of molten steel. The heat is terrific. The glare is very great. After a while, you manage to take a quick look into the vat of boiling steel. You are shocked to see Joe Magarac in the vat.
3. You are a cook in Paul Bunyan's kitchen. You turn over several giant hamburgers. Then you pour a bushel or two of vegetables into the soup. You taste the soup and find that it needs more salt. You add *just a pinch* of salt. After that, you put on a pair of roller skates, pick up a very heavy tray and skate out of the kitchen.
4. With the help of your teacher and some friends, work out a pantomime for a whole story. You might find it easy to pantomime all of *The Strange Armies From the Sky*.
5. Pantomime a single scene from one of the legends in this book. Have your classmates try to guess which character you are playing.